WITHDRAWN
UTSA LIBRARIES

Latin American Inflation

Latin American Inflation

The Structuralist – Monetarist Debate

Susan M. Wachter
University of Pennsylvania

Lexington Books

D.C. Heath and Company
Lexington, Massachusetts
Toronto

Library of Congress Cataloging in Publication Data

Wachter, Susan M.
    Latin American inflation.

    Includes index.
    Bibliography: p.
    1. Inflation (Finance) — Latin America.   2. Money supply—Latin
America. I. Title.
HG660.5.W3   332.4'1'098   75-3820
ISBN 0-669-99622-X

Published simultaneously in Canada

Printed in the United States of America

International Standard Book Number: 0-669-99622-X

Library of Congress Catalog Card Number: 75-3820

To My Parents

Contents

List of Figures

List of Tables

Preface

Inflation has plagued Latin America since the late nineteenth century. Two competing schools of thought have developed in Latin America to explain this chronic inflation. Latin American monetarism suggests that the factors which cause inflation in Latin America are similar to those causing inflation elsewhere and are primarily a matter of excess demand. Overly expansive monetary and fiscal policies are seen as the evils out of which inflation evolves. Roberto Campos has been a major proponent of the Latin American monetarist viewpoint.[1] The classic econometric study embodying monetarist assumptions has been done by Arnold Harberger.[2]

The second theory, structuralism, stresses that there are factors peculiar to Latin America's institutional structure which explain why that region is predisposed to inflation. Here the major proponents include Seers, Prebisch, and Sunkel.[3] Structuralists agree with monetarists that the money supply increases along with the price level. They believe, however, that the money stock is responding to inflation rather than initiating it. The initiating root factors, they hypothesize, are not to be found in monetary and fiscal policies but rather in the more basic weaknesses characteristic of the Latin American economies.

The monetarist and structuralist models differ not only in their basic theories as to what causes inflation but also in the implications of their theories for the relationship between economic growth and inflation. According to the structuralist school, the roots of inflation are in the weaknesses of the agriculture and international trade sectors and/or the income inelasticity of the tax system. Structuralist theory then implies that any economic growth in the presence of these bottlenecks inevitably brings inflation. On the other hand, monetarist theory implies that inflation need not accompany growth; it is suggested, moreover, that due to pervasive government price controls, growth is impeded by inflation.

The debate is not merely academic, for the policy conclusions drawn from the two schools' theories diverge sharply; at various times, Latin American governments have attempted to implement the recommendations of each side of the debate. The anti-inflation policy of the current regimes in Brazil and Chile which includes the application of fiscal and monetary restraint has been influenced by the Brazilian and Chilean proponents of monetarist theory. The land reform programs of both Frei's and Allende's governments in Chile were justified not only in terms of equity and improved agricultural performance but also in terms of the structuralist inflation theory.

As might be expected, a consensus position also exists among Latin American economists which grants both structural and monetarist factors a role in the inflationary process. "Structural problems are considered to be at the root of inflation, but demand problems are clearly related to the propagation and persistence of the phenomenon."[4]   And although structualism was originally formulated to explain inflation in Latin America, several studies have since attempted to apply this approach to the understanding of the inflationary experience in developing countries in other areas. Yet, in spite of this wide-spread (although far from unanimous) acceptance that structural problems can be at the root of an ongoing inflationary process, little attempt has been made either to formulate rigorously or to test the theory. The structuralist approach lacks the theoretical underpinnings needed to compete with the monetarist hypothesis.

The first purpose of this study is to develop a statement of the structuralist hypothesis, specifically of the role of agricultural difficulties in inflation, which can be subjected to hypothesis testing. The second purpose is to test this theory and that of the Latin American monetarists using data from Chile, Argentina, Brazil, and Mexico.

The plan of the book is as follows: Chapter 1 is divided into five sections: Section I summarizes the salient points of the structuralist-monetarist dispute. In Section II some aspects of structuralist theory are reconsidered. Sections III and IV develop an alternative way of formulating the model. Section V examines the relationship between Latin American structuralism and two other nonmonetarist theories of inflation. Chapter 2 describes and evaluates several previous empirical studies on inflation in Latin America. Chapter 3 compares alternative specifications of Latin American monetarism and summarizes the testable hypotheses that arise out of the Latin American monetarist and the reformulated structuralist models. In Chapter 4, the tests are performed, the empirical results analyzed, and the policy implications of the findings are discussed. Chapter 5 provides a summary of the study.

Acknowledgments

I am grateful to many individuals for their assistance in the completion of this book. Professor David Belsley, Professor Huston McCullogh, and Professor Geoffrey Woglom guided my initial efforts and the formulation of the basic ideas. In addition, the book has benefited from the inspiration and guidance of Professor Jere Behrman. I am also grateful to Professor Stephen Ross for his helpful suggestions. Finally, I wish to express my deep gratitude for his substantial help to Professor Michael L. Wachter.

Financial support was provided by the Rodney L. White Foundation for Financial Research at the Wharton School of the University of Pennsylvania. Excellent research assistance was given by Jeffrey Miller, James Orr, Lloyd Buchanan, and Gail Moskowitz. Responsibility for the content of the book is mine alone.

Latin American Inflation

1 The Latin American Monetarist-Structuralist Debate

I. Summary of Latin American Structuralist and Monetarist Theories

Latin American structuralists and monetarists disagree on three related issues: the causes of inflation, the relationship between inflation and growth, and the appropriate policy response to inflation.

I.A. Monetarist Theory

I.A.1. A Summary of Latin American Monetarist Theory. The Latin American monetarist position on the causes of price increases can be summarized briefly since it states in a familiar way that excess demand is responsible for inflation.[1] Hence, the monetarist school is rooted in the belief that increases in money income occur in response to increases in aggregate demand. Inflation is the result of continued expansion of aggregate demand after real income approaches the capacity or supply constraints of the economy. According to Latin American monetarists, this inflation is generated by unjustified expansion both in government deficits (financed for the most part by increases in the money supply) and in central bank loans to the public and to commercial banks. Due to the weakness of government bond markets, little expansion in aggregate demand occurs without concomitant growth in the money supply. Thus, increases in the money supply accompany expansionary fiscal policy as well as expansionary monetary policy. This may explain the origin of the use of the term "monetarist" in Latin America to refer to those who see excess aggregate demand as the cause of inflation.

Latin American monetarists, unlike those identified as monetarists in the United States, do not take a position on the question of whether money supply growth to finance government spending has a greater impact on nominal income than money supply growth to finance central bank loans to the public. Hence, Latin American monetarists are not necessarily claiming that, in theory, only money matters. In this respect they can be distinguished from U.S. monetarists. Since the Latin American monetarist viewpoint stresses the role of aggregate demand, U.S. monetarist theory is a subcategory of this broader approach.

The second element of monetarist theory is its view of the impact of inflation on growth. If wages lag behind prices due to workers' money illusion,

1

and if profit earners invest the increased real earnings this lag allows, increased economic growth can be the result. The monetarists argue, however, that at best this is only a short-run phenomenon. Since money illusion does not persist this cannot be a source of continuing growth. Furthermore, it is felt that negative factors outweigh the positive short-run effect of money illusion. First, in the short run and possibly in the long run as well, inflation is seen as increasing economic uncertainty, with the result that investment and economic growth decline. Second, the traditional government response to inflation is price controls. Monetarists argue that price controls cannot be enforced except at great cost and lead to distortions in the economy which result in inefficiencies and a slower growth of output. For example, interest rate controls are seen as resulting in the reduction and misallocation of investment funds.

Whereas, in developed, stable economies the neoclassical position is that changes in the rate of inflation, in the long run, have minimal real effects, Latin American monetarists argue this is not the case for economies with high rates of inflation and price controls. Hence, for Latin American countries that utilize price controls, the economy in practice is not regarded as inflation neutral.

The following policy prescription is offered by monetarists: To encourage growth, inflation must be ended with a program of monetary and fiscal restraint since it is the lack of such restraint which led to the rising prices. Although the result may be greater price instability, it is often argued that, if inflation is not contained, a second best solution is to end or avoid price controls.

I.A.2. Harberger's Model. For purposes of econometric testing it is necessary to specify more formally the Latin American monetarist model. Harberger, in his study, "The Dynamics of Inflation in Chile,"[2] provides the classical and still the best known version of such a model and tests his hypothesis on Chilean data. As will be seen, Harberger assumes in his model that monetary policy sufficiently dominates fiscal policy in importance so that the latter may be ignored. It is not totally clear whether this view is based on the institutional features of the Chilean economy or on Harberger's attachment to the United States version of the monetarist hypothesis. He also assumes that the economy is at full employment. These assumptions are not specifically called for in the Latin American monetarist viewpoint, and an alternative model of aggregate-demand determined inflation, which does not include these restrictions, is discussed and compared to the Harberger model in Chapter 3. In this section Harberger's model is summarized. The results arrived at from the testing of his model are examined in Chapter 2.

Harberger derives his model of inflation by using the traditional liquidity preference function to express the demand for money. In this view, the demand for money is a function of the price level, the level of real income, and the cost of holding money. The supply of money is then assumed to be determined exogenously. In equilibrium, given the level of real income and the cost of holding money, the price level will adjust to equate the demand for money to an existing supply. Thus the price level is expressed as a function of the quantity of money, the level of real income, and the costs of holding cash. The effects of increases in the money supply on the price level are assumed to occur over time, and, so, money supply enters the equation in the form of a distributed lag. Since Harberger is interested in analyzing the inflation rate rather than the price level he takes percentage first differences of the above described function and arrives at the following:

$$\left(\frac{\dot{P}}{P}\right)_t = a + b\left(\frac{\dot{y}}{y}\right)_t + c\left(\frac{\dot{M}}{M}\right)_t + d\left(\frac{\dot{M}}{M}\right)_{t-1} + e\left(\frac{\dot{A}}{A}\right)_t . \quad (1.1)$$

That is, the inflation rate, $(\dot{P}/P)_t$, is expressed as a function of the percentage change of the quantity of money during the current period, $(\dot{M}/M)_t$, and the past period $(\dot{M}/M)_{t-1}$, the percentage change in real income, $(\dot{y}/y)_t$, and the percentage change in the expected cost of holding cash, $(\dot{A}/A)_t$. In Harberger's version of the Latin American monetarist theory y_t is always equivalent to full-employment output and is thus exogenous. (Alternative monetarist models not incorporating this assumption are discussed in Chapter 3.) Further the cost-of-holding-cash variable, A_t, is not the market rate of return realizable from investment in nonmonetary assets but rather simply a proxy for the expected rate of inflation. That is, the real rate of return is not included in this variable. Harberger ignores the real interest rate, not because he feels it has no influence on the cost of holding cash and therefore on the inflation rate, but rather because of data limitations and because of what he assumes is the lesser influence of this factor in comparison to that of the expected inflation rate. Interest rates on bank loans in Chile are subject to legal control and were usually negative in real terms during this period. Thus they did not offer a measure of the real rate of return on noncash assets. Moreover, Harberger assumes that the expected real rate of return on alternative assets did not vary much in comparison with the volatile movements in the expected rate of inflation so that a measure of the change in cost of holding cash is not significantly affected by ignoring the change in the real rate of return.

To summarize, in Harberger's model, government induced expansion in aggregate demand, assumed to be the result of money supply growth, is the primary cause of a higher price level. The cost of holding cash is assumed to be predetermined and full-employment income is assumed to be exogenous in the inflation process.

I.B. Structuralist Theory[3]

There has been a long history in Latin America of opposition to the demand-pull-oriented monetarist theory. The structuralist approach was first developed in the 1950s by a group of economists centered in Chile and working for the Economic Commission for Latin America.[4] They sought to explain why certain Latin American economies seemed particularly likely to suffer inflation. Structuralism was especially influenced by the Chilean experience of almost a century of inflation, and received impetus out of the failure in Chile to stem inflation through implementing, in 1955, a program of austerity supported by the International Monetary Fund.[5] The intent of the structuralists, however, was to develop a model to explain Latin American inflation in general; and the hypothesis has been applied throughout Latin America.

Structuralists differ in the emphasis they give to various factors. While they agree that monetary expansion is a propagating factor in inflation, they feel that more fundamental, "structural," causes are at the root of the inflationary process. The basic source of rising prices is, in general terms, *the pressure of economic growth on an underdeveloped social and economic structure.* In particular, the agriculture, foreign trade, and government sectors are regarded as suffering from institutional rigidities that cause prices to rise with economic development. In agriculture, the slow growth of productivity, which is often ascribed to an outmoded land-tenure system, is held responsible for rising food prices. In the foreign trade sector, the cause for the depreciation of Latin American currencies is found in lagging foreign demand for primary product exports. Finally, in the public sector, deficits are thought to rise "automatically" with development due to an income inelastic taxation system. This study explores the structuralist hypothesis which is based on agricultural difficulties. However, some consideration is given to the relationship of the other arguments to the agricultural bottleneck hypothesis. Sections I.B.1. and I.B.2. below analyze the agricultural and foreign trade bottleneck hypotheses. Section I.B.3. discusses how structuralists link rising relative prices in these sectors to absolute price increases. A consideration of the argument involving the public sector, which is seemingly very close to the monetarist view, is postponed to Chapter 2 where an empirical study based on this hypothesis is examined. Section I.B.4. summarizes the structuralist theory and policy prescriptions.

I.B.1. The Agriculture Sector. One version of structuralism stresses the role of bottlenecks in agriculture. It is argued that, with economic growth and consequent industrialization, there is increased demand for food and raw material deliveries to the industrial sector; but agricultural output is sluggish and cannot keep pace with the demand at constant prices. Thus, the relative price of food rises over time. The rural socioeconomic structure is most often held responsible for this.[6] Thus, according to David Felix, Osvaldo Sunkel, Julio Olivera, and Dudley Seers,[7] among others, it is the deficient institutional structure in the countryside which limits food production and renders it rigid and unresponsive to demand pressures. In their broad use of the term, supply is "inelastic."

The Impact of the Land-Tenure System.   Specifically structuralists cite land-tenure arrangements as the primary cause for low investment and for the relatively backward production techniques of Latin American agriculture.[8]   The land is divided, predominantly, into *minifundia* and *latifundia*, that is, small peasant plots and large estates. Both are seen as contributing to the problem of a relatively backward, traditional agricultural sector. It is argued that large estates are inefficient because their owners are not "economic men," and so are uninterested in maximizing their money profits. Rather the land is held to enhance the owners' status. Little effort is put into management. Few resources are spent on improving the quality of the land or farming equipment. On the other hand, *minifundia* are not productive because they are too small to be efficiently cultivated and because their peasant owners lack the time and human resources to learn better techniques.

Dudley Seers points out that the source of this system is to be found in Latin America's colonial past:

> The majority of countries show the effects of land grants to the officers of the Conquest, which imposed an alien property-owning class on an Indian population; the remainder reflect the slave-owning plantocracies. Large fractions of the labour force work as tenants or farm labourers or small holders. The upper class consists of large landowners, often absentees.[9]

As long as the population was predominantly rural and self-sufficient in food, and as long as there was accessible land to open up, the structuralists agree that the problem of slow productivity growth in agriculture had little impact on inflation. Once industrialization and urbanization began, principally between the two world wars, demand for marketed food supplies grew; and the sector was incapable of responding.

Joseph Grunwald summarizes the oral tradition of the structuralist school on this point:

> Many of the people who are now in the city obtained a large part of their food requirements directly from the farm on which they worked before they migrated. This additional demand for commercial food products plus the change in the composition of demand due to urbanization plus the demand generated by the rapidly increasing population, can only be satisfied if the agricultural production system is sufficiently elastic to respond rapidly to the demand increases. This, however, is not the case for various reasons of which backward institutional arrangements are the most important.[10]

Maynard's View on the Cause of a Technically Backward Agricultural Sector.   Not all structuralists agree with this interpretation. According to

Geoffrey Maynard, sluggish growth in food output cannot be blamed entirely on the land-tenure system.

He argues that the relatively slow growth of the agriculture sector is due also to government policies which actively encouraged industrialization at the expense of agricultural development.[11] Given these policies, however, Maynard agrees that "a large change in relative prices was required to produce balance between the demand and supply of food"[12] and he concludes with others of this school that "food prices led the way in the great inflations experienced by Latin American countries."[13] In summary, structuralists assume rising relative food prices over time due to the prevailing land-tenure arrangement and, in the argument made by Maynard, to government policy as well. The heart of the structuralist theory is the link that is then drawn between rising relative agricultural prices and overall inflationary pressures. This is discussed in Section I.B.3.

An Analytical Framework. The structuralist model of inflation requires, as is brought out explicitly below, the fulfillment of two assumptions: First, the relative price of food must rise over the long run. Second, prices in agriculture must be more sensitive to excess demand than prices elsewhere in the economy. This latter assumption, which links the rise in food prices to the rise in the overall price level, is examined in Section I.B.3. Here the assumed secular rise of agricultural prices relative to other prices is discussed. To analyze the arguement that agricultural prices are rising relative to other prices over the long run, it is important to relate what is going on in agriculture to the rest of the economy. Such a procedure is usually neglected by structuralists. A base for such an analysis is provided, however, by David Felix:

> A rapid rate of agricultural modernization proved too much for the sluggish organizational structure of the latifundios and the weak investment propensities of the estate owners. Output expansion was slow, food prices pressed upward, and agriculture lost most of its ability to employ the growing population. The result was a heavy influx into the major cities well ahead of the growth of regular job opportunities, to be absorbed in personal services and the casual trades, both legal and illegal, and to be housed in rapidly growing shantytowns and crowded tenements.[14]

This argument is reminiscent of the dual-labor-market model of Lewis,[15] and more recently Harris and Todaro.[16] In order to draw out the implications of rising relative food prices for other prices and wages in the economy it is possible to join the structuralist model to a two-sector labor-surplus model explicitly. To do so, first, assume a model with two sectors: agriculture and manufacturing. Let P_a be an index of food prices; P_m an index of other prices;

W_a an index of wages in agriculture; and W_m wages elsewhere. Whenever excess demand in agriculture is greater than excess demand in manufacturing, P_a rises relative to P_m.[a] Demand in each sector essentially depends on population, P_A, P_M, and income. Supply in each sector depends on commodity prices, input prices, and on technology which is assumed to be autonomously developing over time. Structuralists stress that excess demand in agriculture is greater than excess demand in manufacturing not because demand for food rises relatively faster than demand for industrial output (as would be the case with rising income, if income elasticity of demand for food exceeded that of other goods) but rather because the supply response in agriculture is smaller (as a result of a slower rate of productivity growth) than that found elsewhere. This is due either to institutional inadequacies in agriculture or to government policies which favor industrial growth or to both. If per capita income is increasing (largely as a result of productivity increase in manufacturing) and if population is increasing as well, then demand for industrial and agricultural goods rises. That is, demand curves shift out in both sectors. With productivity increases, supply curves shift out in manufacturing. (There may be *some* shifting out of supply curves in agriculture as well due to productivity increases.) However, productivity increases in agriculture are sufficiently small, relative to those in manufacturing, that excess demand in agriculture is greater than that in manufacturing. Therefore, the relative price of food rises.

It is of interest to see the impact of this process on wages in the two sectors. In essence, although the process begins in the manufacturing sector, wages are likely to go up in both sectors. Due to the increase in demand for manufacturing output coupled with the accumulation of capital and technological changes in the manufacturing sector, there is an increase in demand for labor in that sector. If W_m is greater than W_a, the manufacturing sector may be able to recruit new workers without a further increase in W_m; effectively the higher wage allows the manufacturing sector to hire from a queue. In the dual-labor market models the workers on this queue are identified with the urban unemployed. Alternatively, there are a number of potential factors that may lead to an increase in W_m. First, labor unions may be present in the manufacturing sector and those unions may use the increase in the demand for labor as an opportunity to increase wages. Second, the firms in the manufacturing sector may desire an assured labor

---

[a]This can be shown using a linear price reaction equation, $\dot{P_i}/P_i = K[(D_i - S_i)/S_i)]$, $K > 0$, where $(D_i - S_i)/S_i$ equals the percentage excess demand in the ith market. When the percentage excess demand in agriculture, $(D_A - S_A)/S_A$, is greater than the percentage excess demand in manufacturing, $(D_M - S_M)/S_M$, $(\dot{P}/P)_A$ will be greater than $(\dot{P}/P)_M$, so that the relative price of food, P_A/P_M, rises. In Section III, as part of the reformulated structuralist model, it is shown that K, the price reaction coefficient varies across sectors. Here it is assumed that price reaction coefficients are equal across sectors so that the short-run dynamics path to adjustment can be ignored.

supply and may therefore increase W_m to assure that their increased hiring does not greatly reduce the size of the labor queue. Finally, the new capital or techniques of production may have relatively fixed labor needs and they may require new or additional on-the-job training. Although the firms pay for this training, the workers may still benefit, in the form of higher wages, should firms find it profitable to raise their wages to reduce the turnover of their trained workers.

The increase in W_m and/or the decrease in the amount of urban unemployment leads, *ceteris paribus*, to an increase in the attractiveness of migrating from the agricultural rural areas — which are relatively stagnant and, in any case, suffer from $W_m > W_a$ — to the manufacturing sector. This potential movement off the farm places upward pressure on agricultural prices, P_a, for one of two reasons. First, the agricultural sector can raise W_a to maintain its share of the labor force. Because of the lack of technological change or capital accumulation in this sector, however, the higher wages will lead to higher P_a. Second, if W_a is not increased, the supply of agricultural goods will fall and this will lead to an increase in P_a. Most likely, some combination of the two factors will prevail — with the size of the change in P_a being determined by several factors including the elasticity of the demand for agricultural output.

Summary. With aggregate demand increasing in both sectors, and with technological change and capital accumulation occurring largely in the manufacturing sector, the price of agricultural goods will rise relative to the price of manufacturing goods. The upward movement in P_a/P_m will be greater the larger is the income elasticity of farm goods relative to the income elasticity of manufactured goods and the smaller is the rate of technological change and capital accumulation in agriculture relative to manufacturing.

I.B.2. The Foreign Trade Sector. In theory, the excess demand for agricultural commodities could be satisfied by increased food imports financed by equivalent increases in the value of exports. Structuralists argue, however, that the foreign trade sector is itself deficient, and that, far from being able to lessen agricultural bottlenecks, has its own bottlenecks which contribute to inflationary pressures. Latin American economies often rely primarily on a few commodity exports. It is argued by Seers[17] and others that demand for Latin America's primary product exports on the part of the industrialized economies grows slowly due to low income and price elasticities and to the development of synthetic substitutes. On the other hand, demand for imports in Latin America is seen as income elastic especially since the process of industrialization requires intermediate and capital goods which embody economies of scale that preclude domestic production. For these reasons a tendency exists for the terms of trade to deteriorate. Exchange rate depreciation or increasing controls then raise the price of imports or import substitutes, relative to the price of other nontraded goods.

Those in the structuralist school who discuss both trade and agriculture bottlenecks often consider their effects to be additive.[18] However, it is possible for pressures from these two structuralist sources to cancel each other out in the case of a food exporting economy such as Argentina. If the cause of declining terms of trade is a downward trend in foreign demand for food exports as hypothesized, this results in the slackening of demand for domestically grown food. If supply is not infinitely elastic, the effect of this is a decline in the domestic price of food. This counters the rise in the relative price of food due to agriculture supply problems. Thus the relative rise in the price of food is somewhat mitigated.[b] This canceling effect does not occur in the food exporting economy if the source of the exchange rate depreciation is in a declining domestic supply of food for export rather than in a declining foreign demand for Latin American produced food.[19]

A conflict in the two structuralist hypotheses also does not arise in the case of an economy such as Chile's, which, for the most part, exports nonfood commodities. Here the effect of a tendency for trade deficits is to raise further the relative price of food. If foreign demand for exports increased sufficiently over time, excess demand for food could be satisfied through increased imports paid for by the increased exports without a rise in the relative price of food. If export demand is weak, however, as is hypothesized, an increase in demand for food imports will lead to a depreciation in the exchange rate and a rise in the domestic price of foreign foodstuffs. Hence, a slow growth in demand for nonfood exports makes a relative rise in food prices more likely. The two structuralist arguments complement each other in this case.

I.B.3. Relative and Absolute Price Changes. A relatively backward agricultural sector and foreign exchange bottlenecks are traditional problems of developing economies. The distinguishing feature of the structuralist approach is the argument that these problems can lead to inflation. The monetarist framework assumes either that relative prices do not change or that relative price changes do not influence the rate of inflation. In contrast, for structuralists, the process of adjustment of relative prices affects the absolute price level.

It is clear, however, that the absolute price level does not have to rise for the relative prices of food and imported goods to increase. A rise in the relative price of food or foreign exchange can be accomplished through a decline in prices of other commodities with the overall price level constant.

I.B.3.i. Downward Price Rigidities. One additional and crucial hypothesis made by structuralists which turns relative price increases into overall inflationary pressure is the following: prices in the nonfood, nontrade goods sectors of the

---

[b]It is possible, however, to construct a scenario in which a drop in foreign demand for food exports raises the domestic price of food.

economy are inflexible downward. The role of this assumption is clearly seen in Maynard's discussion of inflation resulting from excess demand in agriculture.[20]

Some go even further and see the sector where the relative price change occurs as unimportant because all prices are assumed to be downwardly rigid. Thus, according to Olivera:

> Although, for purposes of illustration, we initially assumed a change in the direction of demand, it is clear that any movement of relative prices determined by a change in the conditions of supply will similarly produce, if money prices are rigid downwards, an increase of the general price-level.[21]

In general, downward inflexibility of prices is ascribed to the pervasiveness of imperfect competition in those Latin American economies suffering from inflation. The existence of downward price inflexibility due to market power is accepted as an institutional constraint and is not given much attention. Yet it is as crucial to the analysis as are the assumptions of bottlenecks in the agriculture and foreign trade sectors. It is the rise in the relative price of food combined with the rigidity of nonfood prices that results in an increase in the level of prices. This unexamined assumption of downward inflexibility in nonfood prices is a weakness of the structuralist model which is discussed and modified in Sections II and III below.

I.B.3.ii. Spillovers. The structuralist position described above is based on the upward movement of prices in the agriculture sector coupled with the downward rigidity of prices in the nonfarm sector. In addition, structural theorists note that spillovers may cause prices to rise in this latter sector rather than be simply downwardly rigid. This result occurs if unions attempt to recoup, in wage increases, the increase in food prices. This cost-push type of increase in wages creates upward price pressure in manufacturing through an increase in factor costs. This would occur whenever short-run pricing schemes give greater weight to costs and less weight to excess demand conditions. In this way "the initial price increases resulting from import substitution will probably set an inflationary spiral."[22] And agricultural bottlenecks may also provoke such a process:

> With the lack of a supply response from the agricultural sector, food shortages continue. The cost of living of the workers and wages rise. Local manufacturers usually have no trouble in passing on increased costs to consumers. Thus agricultural inelasticity will bring on a spiral of wages and prices.[23]

I.B.4. Summary of the Theory and Policy Prescriptions. To summarize, there are two elements traditionally specified as necessary for structural inflation: first, excess demand in the agricultural and/or foreign traded goods sectors which has the effect of bidding up relative prices in these sectors; second, price and wage floors and/or spillovers in the nonfarm nontraded goods sectors.

If such factors are at the root of inflationary pressures, monetary and fiscal policies can slow the inflation but only at a cost to economic development. With a stagnant agricultural sector, for example, growth elsewhere in the economy will increase the demand for agricultural products (due to an increase in income) while reducing the supply (by drawing away labor resources). This leads to an increase in prices which cannot be offset by decreases in the rigid prices elsewhere in the economy. Hence, the only way to prevent prices from rising is to curtail the increase in excess demand for agricultural and foreign traded goods. Without extensive structural change, this means stopping economic growth. Thus, the preferred way to stop inflation is through structural reforms:

> The second sort of action, with a greater chance of success in Latin America than over-all restrictions upon demand, is the loosening of bottlenecks — that is, of particular insufficiencies in supply that are possible causes of inflationary spiral. Herein lies the role of investments bearing a rapid maturity, of food imports in the event of poor harvests, and of agrarian reforms, doubtless difficult to manage but the effect of which should eventually be the increase of food production and the simultaneous disappearance of both the largest landholdings, where there is no incentive to rational production, and the smallest, whose lack of means restrains development.[24]

In the absence of such reforms, structuralists conclude that price stability is incompatible with economic development.

The traditional structuralist viewpoint outlined here suggests that a backward agriculture sector can cause overall inflationary pressure. Yet the arguement as it stands can be criticized on several specific grounds, as the following Section II points out. More generally, the structuralist approach to inflation has not been rigorously formulated or tested. The purpose of Sections III and IV below is to derive a formal structural inflation model which leads to testable hypotheses.

II. A Critique of the Structuralist Model

Introduction

There are a number of problematical parts to the theory of structuralism. The traditional structuralist argument fails to provide a formal model to explain this principal point: that an increase in the relative price of food leads to an ongoing inflation. Further, several aspects of the intuitive explanation offered are unsatisfactory. These include: first, the lack of an explanation for rising prices in the nonunionized sector which occur in the face of excess supply; second, the necessity for the relative price of food to increase continuously and at an increasing rate if structuralist factors alone are to account for an ongoing and secularly rising inflation rate; third, the assumption of downwardly rigid prices in the manufacturing and service sectors which the structuralists do not justify theoretically; and, fourth, the unspecified or ambiguous role of aggregate demand and the money supply in a long-run theory of structural inflation. Section II.A. discusses the first two of these issues and Section II.B., the third. In Section III, an alternative, short-run structuralist model is developed which takes account of these problems. Section IV deals with the fourth issue, the question of the impact of aggregate demand on structural inflation in the long run, and then, discusses the long run workings of the reformulated structuralist model.

II.A. Some Contradictory Evidence

An important problem with the structuralist model is that several of its implications are empirically unsupported. First, there is some obvious evidence that calls into question the completeness of the structuralist model. It is possible that prices and wages can remain rigid in a unionized sector even in the presence of underutilized capacity and unemployment; but not all industries in the non-food sector of Latin American economies are unionized, and, in many of the organized industries, the unions are relatively weak.[c] The assumption of zero downward flexibility in wages and prices may be hard to justify under these conditions as the discussion in the following section indicates. Moreover, empirically, the problem is not that nonunionized firms, outside of agriculture (e.g., in the service sector), maintain steady prices when excess supply conditions prevail, but rather that they may continue to raise their prices under these circumstances. The assumption of a floor to wages and prices, even if it is acceptable, is not enough to explain rising prices if excess supply exists. An additional hypothesis must be sought to show why competitive firms raise their prices even though demand for their product may be below capacity.

There is a second problematical implication of the structuralist model. It is simply a matter of arithmetic that a rise in relative prices in agriculture, given a floor to prices in other sectors, requires a rise in the general price level. If prices advance due to excess demand in one sector and are not cut in response to excess

---

[c]Of the economies to be examined here, only Argentina has a unionized sector of substantial importance.

supply elsewhere, the price level increases. This combination of events offers an explanation for a once-and-for-all increase in the price level. A constant inflation rate, however, can be explained within the structuralist framework only if relative prices continue to advance.

Furthermore, in several of the inflationary economies of Latin America, including Chile and Argentina, there is a tendency for the rate of inflation itself to rise. For the traditional structuralist model alone to lead to this result, relative food prices would not only need to rise, they would need to rise at an increasing rate. This seems an unreasonable pattern of price change to require. (In Chile and Argentina, relative food prices have increased in the post World War II period. However, there has been no positive trend in the rate of change in relative food prices as required.) In fact the literature is ambiguous on this point. It is sometimes argued that an increase in the rate of change of relative food prices is called for to generate an increase in the inflation rate. There is some resistance to accepting this implication of the structuralist model; so that, at other times, it is asserted that a rise in the level of relative food prices produces an increase in the inflation rate. How this can be so in the context of the model is not made clear.

In sum, the structuralist model cannot account for the evidence of rising prices in nonunionized firms outside of agriculture; further, the model's implication of a continuous increase in relative food prices is not empirically supported. Hence, the traditional structuralist argument is in need of modification if it is to be consistent with observed price movements.

II.B. The Assumption of Downwardly Rigid Prices

An additional problem with the structuralist approach is its reliance on the assumption of downward inflexibility in prices in nonfood sectors in times of excess supply and upward flexibility in times of excess demand. By definition excess supply conditions must exist in the nonfood sectors if it is hypothesized that total aggregate demand is not excessive and that excess demand exists in agriculture. It is not clear, however, why in the face of excess supply conditions, firms in the nonfood sectors maintain rigid prices while increasing prices otherwise. Structuralists ascribe downward price rigidity and upward flexibility to the presence of oligopoly power in the manufacturing and service sectors; but theoretical doubts can be raised about ascribing this asymmetrical pricing response to oligopolistic factors. There is also a problem in adopting the alternative and weaker assumption that prices move up just as readily but adjust more slowly (rather than not move at all) in a downward direction in oligopolistic sectors than they do in *other* sectors.[d] The pricing behavior described by both

---

[d]Victorio Corbo, in his study, *Inflation in Developing Countries* (Amsterdam: North-Holland, 1974), provides, in the case of Chile, additional evidence for questioning the

of these assumptions is not consistent with the maximization of an oligopolistic industry's long-run profits. To see this, assume that an oligopolistic industry is in equilibrium at its profit maximizing price. Now assume that demand increases for just a short period and that this causes the short run profit maximizing price to rise. If oligopolies respond readily to the temporarily increased demand by raising prices, when demand falls, they have the wrong price. The original price now maximizes profits but, by the assumption under question, oligopolies hesitate to lower their prices again. It is quite likely that downward price changes do threaten industrywide pricing discipline. They may be interpreted as an attempt by one firm to increase its market share and so may spark a price war. To avoid this, firms may hesitate to cut prices. However, if firms are slow to lower prices, maximization of profits requires them to hesitate before raising prices as well. Since prices cannot be adjusted downwards without cost, they should be raised only when conditions which call for a price rise will persist. Otherwise firms will be committed to a pricing structure which is too high to maximize current profits. Hence, oligopolies may lag in raising or lowering prices in response to changes in demand, to preserve industrywide cooperation on pricing structure.[25] If firms pursue this strategy the assumption that prices are more likely to move up readily but down slowly in organized sectors must be questioned. This assumption of asymmetrical price responsiveness is not necessary to a structuralist theory of inflation and, in Section III, where the structuralist model is reformulated, it is replaced with the assumption that, on average, firms in manufacturing and service markets are slower to adjust prices in either direction to changed market conditions than those in the agriculture sector.

Conclusion. The structuralist model is stated in an intuitive form. Consequently, it is unclear how one would go about testing it. Related to this is the fact that structuralism specifies no role either for inflationary expectations[26] or for aggregate demand elements, and so it is incomplete as a model of inflation. The reformulated structuralist model, derived in Sections III and IV, attempts to deal with these problems as well as to answer the specific criticisms of the traditional structuralist model raised in this section. Far from invalidating the basic point of the structuralist approach, once inflationary expectations and aggregate demand elements are included, it is possible to avoid the problems outlined above. In particular, structuralist factors can be linked to an ongoing

---

assumption that prices adjust more slowly downwards than upwards. He estimates an inflation equation, for Chile, with capacity utilization as an independent variable. He argues, for the greater downward inflexibility hypothesis to be true, a smaller coefficient of this variable would be expected in times of slack than in the rest of the period. His evidence rejects this hypothesis.

inflation process without the need to assume either a floor to price changes in the nonunionized, oligopolistic sector or a continual rise in the relative price of food.

III. Structuralism Reformulated

Introduction

The purpose of this section is to derive the structuralist hypothesis that relative prices affect the inflation rate from a clearly specified theoretical framework which provides refutable hypotheses and which answers the specific criticisms of the traditional structuralist approach raised in the previous sections. The model is briefly outlined in III.A. and then is derived and stated in a more rigorous form in III.B.1. and III.B.2. In presenting the argument in functional notation, use is made of an article: Enthoven, "Monetary Disequilibria and the Dynamics of Inflation."[27] This is summarized in Section III.B.1. Section III.B.2. extends Enthoven's analysis to present the structuralist argument in an explicit analytical framework and to integrate the argument into a macroeconomic model stressing the role of aggregate demand. The macroeconomic model used as a foundation for the structuralist theory derived in this section is the Harberger quantity theory of money model of inflation described previously in Section I.A.2. The structuralist model of inflation is synthesized with alternative formulations of aggregate demand oriented models of inflation in Chapter 3.

III.A.   The Reformulated Structuralist Model: An Overview

This section briefly describes a simple model of inflation. The framework includes expectation and demand elements as well as structuralist factors.

In economies with persistent inflation, it is reasonable to assume that individuals anticipate a positive future rate of inflation. Thus it is likely that individuals use some model to formulate their expectations of future rates of price change. Now assume that in some way the government is able to increase money aggregate demand to validate the expected price increases (as discussed further below). Then, in equilibrium, real demand and supply of goods are in balance and prices increase at the expected rate of inflation. Money aggregate demand increases just enough to support the expected increase in prices and any rise in real aggregate supply, so that the actual rate of inflation equals the expected rate. Assuming that all markets experience zero excess demand conditions, the expected and actual rate of price change in all sectors continues unchanged. The overall inflation rate also is constant and no other explanation for inflation is necessary. Excess demand, in real terms, in any given sector would cause prices to rise further than the expected rate in that sector. And similar conditions of excess supply in other sectors would cause prices there to rise but at a slower than equilibrium rate.

Although this simple expectational model can explain an unchanging rate of inflation, changes in the rate of inflation still need to be explained. Monetarists would attribute a rise in the overall inflation rate to an increased rate of growth of aggregate demand. It would seem that if the expansion in money aggregate demand is kept equal to the real growth in output plus the expected growth in prices, inflation would continue at the equilibrium expected rate. However, this is not necessarily the case. Overall demand may be kept in balance with an increase in demand in one sector balancing a decrease in another. Different sectors then may adjust their prices to changes in the level of demand at different speeds.[e] Competitive sectors may adjust their prices and wages in reaction to changed demand conditions faster than noncompetitive sectors. First, unionized industries in the noncompetitive sectors are more likely to be committed contractually, in the short run, to a given percentage wage increase even though current demand makes the wage rise inappropriately low or high. Second, even in the absence of a union imposed floor to wage cuts, oligopolistic industries may choose to change their price structure less often than competitive industries. As was indicated above, the long-run optimal pricing strategy for an oligopolistic industry may be to move slowly in adjusting prices and wages in response to positive and negative fluctuations in excess demand.

Furthermore, even without market power, some industries may adjust prices more slowly than others. This may occur because the nature of the goods they sell, for example, housing, requires the setting of prices for relatively fixed contract periods.[f] Thus assuming overall demand equals overall supply but that

---

[e]Unlike in the traditional view, in the model outlined here prices are assumed to move more slowly in non-food sectors than in food sectors in both directions, not merely in a downward direction, and zero downward flexibility in non-food prices is not assumed. Thus, the only assumption required here is that prices are more flexible, for whatever reason, in the agricultural sector than elsewhere.

[f]There is another explanation for a lagged adjustment of prices to excess demand conditions in organized and, to a lesser extent, in competitive industries. In unionized firms and even in many nonunion firms, wages of employees are altered only at discrete intervals—generally once a year. The explanation for this wage setting process in unionized firms is related to the fixed term, wage contract. Even where escalator clauses are present, the wage rate is adjusted with a time lag, again at regular time intervals fixed by the contract, and often by an incomplete amount to compensate for the rise in prices. In nonunionized firms as well, it is costly for employers to inform employees of pay changes at short intervals. This involves direct pecuniary costs of setting the wage and notifying everyone of the changes and the indirect or non-pecuniary costs related to the inevitable morale problems which arise whenever wages are changed. Prices may then be set to some extent as a mark-up on wages. Thus, if an industry's labor value added is high, prices may be slower to adjust than in an industry with lower labor added value. One would expect, however, that wages and prices are set more frequently in competitive firms, and thus, on these grounds also, that prices are more flexible in competitive than in organized sectors.

the composition of demand is such that there is an increase in demand in sectors where prices adjust rapidly, such as agriculture, and a corresponding decrease in demand elsewhere in the economy, the inflation rate in the short run would rise. But this is just what the structuralists argue is occurring. The basic assumption of the structuralist view is that with economic growth in the presence of a lagging agricultural sector, the increasing demand for agricultural products overruns supply increases in that sector. Even in an economy without inflationary expectations or excessive aggregate demand, prices in agriculture rise as a result of the excess demand in that sector. The matching excess supply occurring in the non-food sectors may not lead to a balancing decline in wages and prices. Demand would be less than supply but prices would not fall there at the same rate that they rise in the agricultural sector. In the extreme case, prices rise in agriculture due to excess demand in that sector but, in spite of excess supply, prices in the rest of the economy remain unchanged. The overall result, in the *short run*, is a rise in the price level. A validating monetary policy is necessary if this rise in prices is to be maintained in the long run.

In an economy with inflationary expectations and ratification of these expectations by monetary and fiscal authorities, exogenous changes in sectoral balances result in short-run shifts in the inflation rate. For example, given an ongoing inflation, excess demand in agriculture leads to a food price increase at a rate which is greater than the expected inflation rate. However, balancing excess supply elsewhere does not cause an equal drop in the rate of price change. Hence, the overall inflation rate rises. Again this is a short-run result unless the acceleration in the inflation rate is validated by monetary authorities.

Furthermore, developing economies such as those of Latin America may be subject to upward relative price pressure in the agricultural sector due to the difficulties of modernizing this traditional sector. To the extent they are, they would be more prone to inflationary pressures than developed countries where excess demand might not be expected to occur systematically in agriculture.[g]

In summary, sectoral imbalances as well as increasing aggregate demand can cause a short-run spurt in prices or in the inflation rate. Sections III.B.1 and III.B.2 develop an explicit statement of this short-run model for an economy with a zero expected inflation rate. The model is extended to an economy with inflationary expectations in Chapter 3. As Section IV of this chapter indicates, a passive money supply must be introduced into the model if the new higher price level or inflation rate is to persist in the long run.

III.B. A Theoretical Framework

III.B.1. A Summary of Enthoven's Analysis. The purpose of this section is

---

[g]In a world with imperfect mobility and tariffs and quantity restraints on international trade, the level of and movements in relative prices of food do not have to be similar across economies, although they may be at times.

to summarize Enthoven's study, "Monetary Disequilibria and the Dynamics of Inflation."[28] His conclusions are then extended, in Section III.B.2., to present, in functional form, the reformulated structuralist theory, discussed in Section III.A. above. In developing this theory, the first problem is to prove that excess aggregate demand and more specifically what may be termed the Keynes-Hansen condition for inflationary pressure is neither necessary nor sufficient for a rise in prices. It is shown that, under various reasonable assumptions, the price level depends not only on the level of excess aggregate demand but on the composition of aggregate demand as well. In demonstrating this, first, a Walrasian expression, which is used to indicate the level of excess aggregate demand, is introduced. Second, a price reaction equation is defined. Finally, using the Laspeyres price index, necessary and sufficient conditions for a rise in the price index are derived.

Excess Aggregate Demand: The Keynes-Hansen Condition for Inflation. As expressed in Walras' Law, the net monetary excess demand for all goods is equivalent to an equal excess supply of money. In symbols:

$$\sum_{i=1}^{n} P_i X_i = -X_{n+1} \tag{1.2}$$

where P_i is the price and X_i the excess demand of the ith good. The $n+1$ commodity is money, and $P_{n+1} = 1$. Excess demand equations then take the following form:

$$X_i = X_i(P_1, \ldots, P_n; P_1^e, \ldots, P_n^e; A) \tag{1.3}$$

where P_i^e indicates the expected price, and A is a term representing the initial level and distribution of assets. When there is excess aggregate demand, by definition,

$$\sum_{i=1}^{n} P_i X_i > 0. \tag{1.4}$$

Enthoven defines (1.4) as the Keynes-Hansen criterion for the existence of inflationary pressure. However, once dynamic assumptions about the reaction of prices to excess demand are introduced, the fulfillment of the Keynes-Hansen criterion, i.e., the existence of excess aggregate demand, is shown to be neither necessary nor sufficient for a rise in the Laspeyres price index. The composition of aggregate demand matters as well.

The Price Reaction Equation. The following price reaction equation is assumed in Enthoven's analysis:

$$\frac{\dot{P}_i}{P_i} = \frac{K_i X_i}{q^S_i} = \frac{K_i (q^D_i - q^S_i)}{q^S_i} \tag{1.5}$$

where $\dot{P}_i$ is the first derivative of the price of good i with respect to time, K_i, a positive constant, X_i, the level of excess demand,[h] q^D_i, the quantity demanded, and q^S_i, the quantity supplied. The equation states that the relative rate of change in a price is directly proportional to the excess demand for the good expressed as a fraction of the quantity supplied.

Necessary and Sufficient Conditions for a Rise in the Price Level. Following Enthoven, one can use (1.5) to derive necessary and sufficient conditions for a rise in the Laspeyres price index, P_L, the price index which is in general use:[i]

$$P_L = \frac{\sum_{i=1}^{n} \bar{q}_i P_i}{\sum_{i=1}^{n} \bar{q}_i \bar{P}_i} \tag{1.6}$$

where $\bar{P}_i$ and $\bar{q}_i$ represent prices and quantities in the base period and P_i, current prices. Differentiating P_L with respect to time,

$$\dot{P}_L = \frac{\sum_{i=1}^{n} \bar{q}_i \dot{P}_i}{\sum_{i=1}^{n} \bar{q}_i \bar{P}_i} . \tag{1.7}$$

Substituting (1.5) into (1.7),

---

[h] $\dot{P}_i/P_i$, the rate of change of prices in the ith sector, is thus defined to be a function of X_i. As defined by Enthoven in equation (1.3), X_i depends on expected prices as well as actual prices and assets. It is possible to separate out the influence of expected prices and have $\dot{P}_i/P_i$ a function of the expected inflation rate, $\dot{P}_e/P_e$, and a redefined excess demand variable Z_i which excludes the impact of expectational elements. This is discussed in Chapter 3.

[i] A Paasche index could also be used, since Enthoven assumes, implicitly, that the quantity weights are frequently updated.

$$\dot{P}_L \; = \; \frac{\sum\limits_{i=1}^{n} \bar{q}_i P_i K_i \dfrac{X_i}{q_i^s}}{\sum\limits_{i=1}^{n} \bar{q}_i \bar{P}_i} \; \approx \; \frac{\sum\limits_{i=1}^{n} P_i K_i X_i}{\sum\limits_{i=1}^{n} \bar{q}_i \bar{P}_i} \; . \tag{1.8}$$

Equation (1.8) holds precisely for the case when the quantity weights, $\bar{q}_i$, equal the quantities supplied, q_i^s.[j]

For the price level to rise, i.e., for $\dot{P}_L > 0$, the numerator of (1.8) must be positive. (The denominator of (1.8) is always positive.) That is,

$$\sum_{i=1}^{n} P_i K_i X_i > 0 \tag{1.9}$$

must hold. If the price reaction coefficients, K_i, were the same in all sectors, (1.9) would reduce to

$$K \sum_{i=1}^{n} P_i X_i > 0 , \tag{1.10}$$

so that when inflation occurs, the following holds:

$$\sum_{i=1}^{n} P_i X_i > 0 . \tag{1.4}$$

The Keynes-Hansen criterion for inflationary pressure, that is, excess aggregate demand, would have to be fulfilled for a rise in prices. Once the K_is vary among sectors, however, the distribution of aggregate demand as well as its level affects the price level. The inflation rate is no longer a function of the level of excess aggregate demand (1.4) alone.[k]

---

[j]This assumption which essentially requires the quantity weights to equal the current quantities supplied is maintained throughout Section III. The assumption simplifies the exposition but is not necessary for the testing of the model. It is relaxed in Chapter 4 when the weighting schemes in actual use in the computation of price indices for the economies considered here are discussed.

[k]This holds in the short run before prices adjust to clear all markets. If the K_i are sufficiently large so that prices adjust to market clearing levels sufficiently quickly in all sectors, the return to overall equilibrium may occur, for example, within the quarter. Then quarterly price level data are affected only by the level of excess aggregate demand and not by its distribution.

III.B.2. An Analytical Framework for Short-run Structural Inflation. Although Enthoven has not developed his model for this purpose, his analysis can be adapted to provide a theoretical underpinning for the structuralist hypothesis that excess demand in agriculture contributes to inflationary pressure in the short run. To do so it is necessary to show first how the inflation rate may be functionally related to the presence of excess agricultural demand, given zero excess aggregate demand. This is the object of Section III.B.2.i. Section III.B.2.ii. then shows that when excess demand is higher in agriculture than elsewhere, the relative price of food rises. This second result is used in deriving the reformulated structuralist model as a testable hypothesis. In the model derived in Sections III.B.2.i. and III.B.2.ii., it is assumed that excess aggregate demand equals zero. In Section III.B.2.iii, this assumption is relaxed.

III.B.2.i. The Short-Run Impact of Excess Demand in Agriculture on Inflation. The analysis of Section III.B.1 may be used to derive theoretically a foundation for the structuralist model. Specifically, given zero excess demand in the overall economy, positive excess demand in the agriculture sector (assuming prices there are more flexible than elsewhere) can generate increases in the price level in the short run. This is seen by dividing the economy into two sectors, identifying P_1 and q_1 as the price and output of the agricultural sector and P_2 and q_2 as price and output in the nonagricultural sector. The Laspeyres price index in period t can then be written:

$$P_L(t) = \frac{\bar{q}_1 P_1(t) + \bar{q}_2 P_2(t)}{\bar{q}_1 \bar{P}_1 + \bar{q}_2 \bar{P}_2} \quad , \tag{1.11}$$

where $\bar{q}_1$ and $\bar{q}_2$ and $\bar{P}_1$ and $\bar{P}_2$ are base period quantities and prices, respectively, and $P_1(t)$ and $P_2(t)$ are current prices. The change in the Laspeyres price index over a given period is,

$$
\begin{aligned}
\dot{P}_L(t) &= P_L(t) - P_L(t\text{-}1) \\[2mm]
&= \frac{\bar{q}_1 P_1(t) + \bar{q}_2 P_2(t)}{\bar{q}_1 \bar{P}_1 + \bar{q}_2 \bar{P}_2} - \frac{\bar{q}_1 P_1(t\text{-}1) + \bar{q}_2 P_2(t\text{-}1)}{\bar{q}_1 \bar{P}_1 + \bar{q}_2 \bar{P}_2} \tag{1.12} \\[2mm]
&= \frac{\bar{q}_1 \dot{P}_1(t) + \bar{q}_2 \dot{P}_2(t)}{\bar{q}_1 \bar{P}_1 + \bar{q}_2 \bar{P}_2} \quad .
\end{aligned}
$$

Using the price reaction equation,

$$\frac{\dot{P}_i}{P_i} = \frac{K_i X_i}{q_i^S} \tag{1.5}$$

and, for purposes of simplicity, defining $G = \bar{q}_1 \bar{P}_1 + \bar{q}_2 \bar{P}_2$, it can be shown that

$$\dot{P}_L = \left(\frac{\bar{q}_1 P_1 K_1 X_1}{q_1^S} + \frac{\bar{q}_2 P_2 K_2 X_2}{q_2^S} \right) \Big/ G . \tag{1.13}$$

The qs in (1.13) cancel out, maintaining the assumption that the base weights equal the quantities supplied, so that, in this case,

$$\dot{P}_L = \frac{K_1 P_1 X_1 + K_2 P_2 X_2}{G} . \tag{1.14}$$

If $P_1 X_1 = -P_2 X_2$, and, as the structuralist argument assumes, if $K_1 > K_2$, then $\dot{P}_L$ is positive. Hence, the price level rises in spite of the absence of excessive aggregate demand.

Equation (1.14) can be taken further to derive the following result: Assume $K_1 > K_2$ and zero excess demand in the overall economy. Then the larger excess demand is in agriculture (with balancing excess supply elsewhere), the larger is $K_1 P_1 X_1 + K_2 P_2 X_2$ and, therefore the greater is $\dot{P}_L$. To show this, assume a two-period model. In period t, the economy is in equilibrium so that,

$$X_1(t) = X_2(t) = 0 \tag{1.15}$$

and

$$\dot{P}_1(t) = \dot{P}_2(t) = \dot{P}_L(t) = 0 . \tag{1.16}$$

Equilibrium prices in the two sectors, $P_1(t)$ and $P_2(t)$, and the overall price level, $P_L(t)$, all measured, at the end of period t, prevail. That is, prices have not changed over period t and are under no pressure to change since excess demands equal zero. Excess demands then differ from zero in period $t + 1$ in a way which causes the price level to rise over that period. To analyze this rise in prices, it is useful to adopt the convention of distinguishing between events that occur immediately at the beginning of period $t + 1$ and events that occur over $t + 1$. In particular, it is assumed that $P_1(t)$ and $P_2(t)$, the prices that prevailed at the end of period t, are substantially unchanged at the opening of $t + 1$, while X_1 and X_2 are free to change immediately at the start of the period.[1]

An exogenous change occurs at the beginning of period $t + 1$, such that

$$X_1(t+1) > 0 \,, \quad X_2(t+1) < 0 \tag{1.17}$$

and

$$P_1(t)X_1(t+1) \;+\; P_2(t)X_2(t+1) \;=\; 0 \,. \tag{1.18}$$

Hence, it is assumed that excess aggregate demand in the beginning of $t + 1$ (based on the unchanged P_i of period t) is equal to zero. The price change over period $t + 1$ is defined as

$$\dot{P}_L(t+1) \;=\; [\dot{P}_1(t+1)\bar{q}_1 \;+\; \dot{P}_2(t+1)\bar{q}_2] \;/\; G \,. \tag{1.19}$$

Price reaction equation (1.5),

$$\frac{\dot{P}_i}{P_i}(t+1) \;=\; \frac{\dot{P}_i(t+1)}{P_i(t)} \;=\; \frac{K_i X_i(t+1)}{q_i^S(t)} \tag{1.5}$$

can then be used to substitute $[K_i P_i(t) X_i(t+1)] \,/\, [q_i^S(t)]$ for $\dot{P}_i(t+1)$ in equation (1.19) to find the change in the price level as a function of excess demand in agriculture.

Then,

$$\dot{P}_L(t+1) \;=\; [K_1 P_1(t)X_1(t+1) \;+\; K_2 P_2(t)X_2(t+1)] \;/\; G \,. \tag{1.20}$$

Since, by the assumptions implicit in (1.17) and (1.18),

$$P_1(t)X_1(t+1) \;=\; -P_2(t)X_2(t+1) \,, \tag{1.21}$$

---

[1]In equilibrium, prices adjust to reduce excess demand in each market to zero. In an economy with inflationary expectations, prices adjust continuously. The value of assets (due to an accommodating monetary and fiscal policy), expected prices, and actual prices may all rise at once. Thus, as indicated by equation (1.3), in a market with zero X_i to begin with, $X_i = f(P_1, \ldots, P_n; P_1^e, \ldots, P_n^e; A)$ remains zero as all arguments of equation (1.3) change proportionally. Excess aggregate demand need not appear for inflation in this case. The model outlined here is extended to describe an economy with non-zero inflationary expectations in Chapter 3. Here, zero inflationary expectations are assumed.

substituting for $P_2\,(t)\,X_2\,(t+1)$ in (1.20), the result is,

$$\dot{P}_L\,(t+1) \;=\; [(K_1 - K_2)\,P_1\,(t)\,X_1\,(t+1)] \;/\; G > 0 \;. \tag{1.22}$$

So that, the higher $X_1\,(t+1)$ is, given that $K_1 > K_2$, the higher is $\dot{P}_L\,(t+1)$.

The above analysis supports the verbal argument in Section III.A.: When excess demand exists in agriculture, $P_1\,X_1 > 0$, balanced by an equivalent excess supply elsewhere, $P_2\,X_2 < 0$, the price level rises; the larger the excess demand in agriculture is, the larger the rise in prices. This follows because prices react more quickly in agriculture than elsewhere. Equation (1.22) also implies, *mutatis mutandis*, that when excess supply exists in agriculture, $P_1\,X_1 < 0$, the price level should fall, and the larger the excess supply in absolute value, the greater the implied decline in the price level in the short run.

III.B.2.ii. The Change in the Relative Food Price as a Measure of the Quantity of Excess Demand in Agriculture. The second object of this section is to indicate that the quantity of excess demand in agriculture, $X_1\,(t)$, can be reflected in the percentage rate of change in the relative price of food, $\psi\,(t)$. In this case, $\psi(t)$ can serve as a proxy for $X_1\,(t)$ in predicting $\dot{P}_L\,(t)$. This is shown by the following: By definition,

$$\psi \;=\; \frac{d\dfrac{P_1}{P_2}}{\dfrac{dt}{\dfrac{P_1}{P_2}}} \;=\; \frac{\dot{P}_1}{P_1} - \frac{\dot{P}_2}{P_2}\;; \tag{1.23}$$

then substituting (1.5) into (1.23),

$$\psi \;=\; \frac{K_1\,X_1}{q_1} \;-\; \frac{K_2\,X_2}{q_2}\;. \tag{1.24}$$

Where $P_1\,X_1 + P_2\,X_2 = 0$, for given prices, P_1 and P_2, the larger X_1 is, the smaller is X_2. Therefore, a positive X_1 implies a positive ψ, and a rise in the relative price of food.[m] The larger X_1 is, the larger is ψ, the percentage change in the relative price of food. Thus ψ reflects the extent of excess demand in

---

[m]More formally, by assumption,

$$P_1\,X_1 \;=\; -P_2\,X_2. \tag{i}$$

agriculture. Then, the structuralist theory that excess demand in agriculture causes a rise in the price level implies, as a testable hypothesis, that $\dot{P}_L$ and ψ move together.

III.B.2.iii. Varying the Assumption of Zero Excess Aggregate Demand. In Sections III.B.2.i. and III.B.2.ii., it has been assumed that

$$\sum_{i=1}^{n} P_i X_i = 0.$$

In this section, first, the above version of the structuralist model is modified to allow for the case where excess aggregate demand differs from zero. Second, the relationship between excess demand in agriculture and the rate of change in the relative price of food is discussed, with the assumption of zero excess aggregate demand relaxed.

To show the impact on the structuralist model of varying the value of excess aggregate demand, assume that

$$P_1 X_1 + P_2 X_2 = a . \tag{1.25}$$

Once again, using the definition of the Laspeyres price index and the price reaction equation (1.5), the result is:

$$\dot{P}_L (t) = \frac{K_1 P_1 (t-1) X_1 (t) + K_2 P_2 (t-1) X_2 (t)}{G} . \tag{1.20}$$

Solving (1.25) for $P_2 X_2$ in terms of $P_1 X_1$ and substituting into (1.20):

Therefore,

$$X_2 = -\frac{P_1 X_1}{P_2}. \tag{ii}$$

Substituting (ii) into the definition for ψ,

$$\psi = \frac{K_1 X_1}{q_1^S} - \frac{K_2}{q_2^S} \left(\frac{-P_1 X_1}{P_2} \right) = \frac{K_1 X_1}{q_1^S} + \frac{K_2}{q_2^S} \frac{P_1}{P_2} X_1 \tag{iii}$$

$$= \left(\frac{K_1}{q_1^S} + \frac{K_2}{q_2^S} \frac{P_1}{P_2} \right) X_1.$$

Since all terms in the coefficient of X_1 are positive, a positive X_1 implies a positive ψ.

$$\dot{P}_L(t) = \frac{K_1 P_1 (t-1) X_1 (t) + K_2 [a(t) - P_1 (t-1) X_1 (t)]}{G} , \quad (1.26)$$

then,

$$\dot{P}_L(t) = \frac{K_2 a(t)}{G} + \frac{(K_1 - K_2) P_1 (t-1) X_1 (t)}{G} . \quad (1.27)$$

The change in the price level in period t, thus, in the general case, depends on the level of excess aggregate demand in that period, and, if K_1 differs from K_2, also on the distribution of excess demand between the two sectors. When $a = 0$, equation (1.27) reduces to the previously discussed (1.22). When $K_1 = K_2$, excess aggregate demand alone determines the change in the price level. In the structuralist theory it is assumed that prices react more quickly in agriculture than elsewhere. K_1 is assumed greater than K_2. Therefore, for any given level of excess aggregate demand, the greater the value of excess demand in agriculture, the greater is the rise in the overall price level.

Equation (1.27) shows $\dot{P}_L$, the change in the price level, as a function of terms representing aggregate demand and excess demand in agriculture. In order to express $\dot{P}_L / P_L$, the rate of inflation, as a function of these variables, both sides of (1.27) are divided by the price level:

$$\frac{\dot{P}_L}{P_L}(t) = \frac{\dot{P}_L(t)}{P_L(t-1)} = \frac{K_2 a(t)}{GP_L(t-1)} + \frac{(K_1 - K_2) P_1 (t-1) X_1 (t)}{GP_L(t-1)} ,$$

$$(1.28)$$

which, using the definition of G given in equation (1.11), results in:

$$\frac{\dot{P}_L}{P_L}(t) = \frac{K_2 a(t)}{P_1 (t-1) \bar{q}_1 + P_2 (t-1) \bar{q}_2} + \frac{(K_1 - K_2) P_1 (t-1) X_1 (t)}{P_1 (t-1) \bar{q}_1 + P_2 (t-1) \bar{q}_2} .$$

$$(1.29)$$

The inflation rate is positively related, first, to the current level of excess aggregate demand relative to output, and, second, assuming $K_1 > K_2$, to excess demand in agriculture relative to overall output.

The second purpose of this section is to indicate the relationship between the quantity of excess demand in agriculture, X_1, and the rate of change in the relative price of food, ψ, in the more general case of variable excess aggregate demand. To do this, again, let

$$P_1 X_1 + P_2 X_2 = a. \tag{1.25}$$

Then, solving for $P_2 X_2$ in terms of $P_1 X_1$ and substituting into (1.24) results in:

$$\psi = \frac{K_1}{q_1^S} X_1 - \frac{K_2}{q_2^S} \left(\frac{a}{P_2} - \frac{P_1}{P_2} X_1 \right) \tag{1.30}$$

or,

$$\psi = \left(\frac{K_1}{q_1^S} + \frac{K_2}{q_2^S} \frac{P_1}{P_2} \right) X_1 - \frac{K_2 \, a}{q_2^S P_2} . \tag{1.31}$$

Letting,

$$e = \cfrac{1}{\cfrac{K_1}{q_1^S} + \cfrac{K_2}{q_2^S} \cfrac{P_1}{P_2}} > 0, \tag{1.32}$$

and,

$$f = \cfrac{K_2 \ / \ q_2^S P_2}{\cfrac{K_1}{q_1^S} + \cfrac{K_2}{q_1^S} \cfrac{P_1}{P_2}} > 0, \tag{1.33}$$

then,

$$X_1 = e \, \psi + f a. \tag{1.34}$$

Substituting (1.34) into (1.27),

$$\dot{P}_L = \frac{K_2 a}{G} + \frac{(K_1 - K_2) P_1}{G} [e \, \psi + fa]. \tag{1.35}$$

or,

$$\dot{P}_L = \frac{[K_2 + f P_1 (K_1 - K_2)]}{G} a + \frac{(K_1 - K_2) P_1 \, e}{G} \psi . \tag{1.36}$$

To relate the inflation rate, $\dot{P}_L / P_L$, to excess aggregate demand and to the rate of change of the relative price of food, both sides of equation (1.36) are divided by the price level. Then,

$$\frac{\dot{P}_L}{P_L} = \frac{[K_2 + fP_1(K_1 - K_2)]}{P_L G} a + \frac{(K_1 - K_2)P_1 e}{P_L G} \psi \qquad (1.37)$$

which again, using equation (1.11), results in:

$$\frac{\dot{P}_L}{P_L} = \frac{[K_2 + fP_1(K_1 - K_2)]}{P_1 \bar{q}_1 + P_2 \bar{q}_2} a + \frac{(K_1 - K_2)P_1 e}{P_1 \bar{q}_1 + P_2 \bar{q}_2} \psi. \qquad (1.38)$$

If K_1 and K_2 are positive, the value of the coefficient of a in equation (1.38) is positive, since $0 < fP_1 < 1$.[n] Thus, the inflation rate varies directly with the

---

[n]By definition

$$f = \frac{K_2/q_2^S P_2}{\dfrac{K_1}{q_1^S} + \dfrac{K_2}{q_2^S} \dfrac{P_1}{P_2}} \qquad (i)$$

Multiplying the numerator and denominator of (i) by $q_2^S P_2 q_1^S$, results in:

$$f = \frac{K_2 q_1^S}{K_1 q_2^S P_2 + K_2 q_1^S P_1}. \qquad (ii)$$

Then, multiplying (ii) by P_1,

$$P_1 f = \frac{K_2 q_1^S P_1}{K_1 q_2^S P_2 + K_2 q_1^S P_1} \qquad (iii)$$

which is, assuming K_1 and K_2 greater than zero, positive and less than 1. Let $h = K_2 + fP_1(K_1 - K_2)$, the coefficient of $a/(P_1 \bar{q}_1 + P_2 \bar{q}_2) = \Sigma P_i X_i / \Sigma P_i \bar{q}_i$, excess demand relative to output. Then

$$h = \frac{K_2 q_1 P_1}{K_1 q_2 P_2 + K_2 q_1 P_1} K_1 + \left(1 - \frac{K_2 q_1 P_1}{K_1 q_2 P_2 + K_2 q_1 P_1}\right) K_2. \qquad (iv)$$

Essentially h equals a weighted sum of the K's, where the weights are each sectors' share of output. Over time h may decline. This may occur because fP_1 varies with agriculture's level of excess aggregate demand. Since $P_1 e > 0$,[o] the value of the coefficient of ψ in (1.38) is positive, negative, or zero depending on whether K_1 is greater than, less than or equal to K_2. If the structuralist hypothesis that $K_1 > K_2$ is correct, the rate of inflation moves with the rate of change in the relative price of food. On the other hand, if $K_2 > K_1$, the rate of change in the price level should be negatively related to the rate of change in the relative price of food.[p] A third possibility is that $K_1 = K_2$, and thus, that $\dot{P}_L/P_L$ is unrelated to the rate of change in the relative price of food.

The sign of the coefficient of ψ depends only on the size of K_1 relative to K_2. The absolute size of the coefficient of ψ approaches in the limit the share of sector 1 in the price index, as K_2 approaches zero.[q]

---

share of output, given K_1 and K_2. If agriculture's share of output declines, and $K_1 > K_2$, the value of h declines. (If $K_1 = K_2$, this has no impact on h.) This implies the reasonable result that, because of the growing importance of the sector where prices react more slowly, a given amount of excess aggregate demand relative to output has less of an immediate impact on the inflation rate.

[o]By definition,

$$e = \frac{1}{\dfrac{K_1}{q_1^S} + \dfrac{K_2}{q_2^S}\dfrac{P_1}{P_2}} .$$ (i)

Multiplying the numerator and denominator of (i) by $q_2^S P_2 q_1^S$ results in:

$$e = \frac{q_2^S P_2 q_1^S}{K_1 q_2^S P_2 + K_2 q_1^S P_1} .$$ (ii)

Then,

$$P_1 e = \frac{P_1 q_1^S P_2 q_2^S}{K_1 q_2^S P_2 + K_2 q_1^S P_1}$$ (iii)

which is, assuming positive K_1 and K_2, greater than zero.

[p]That is, if sector 1 is one in which it is assumed prices adjust more slowly than elsewhere in the economy, the coefficient of the rate of change of prices in sector 1 relative to prices elsewhere should be negative.

[q]To show this let ν equal the coefficient of ψ. That is,

$$\nu = (K_1 - K_2)\frac{P_1 e}{P_1 \bar{q}_1 + P_2 \bar{q}_2} .$$ (i)

Equation (1.38) states that the inflation rate varies directly with excess aggregate demand relative to output, and also with the rate of change of the relative price of food.[r] Harberger's inflation equation,

$$\frac{\dot{P}}{P}(t) = a + b\frac{\dot{y}}{y}(t) + c\frac{\dot{M}}{M}(t) + d\frac{\dot{M}}{M}(t-1) + e\frac{\dot{A}}{A}(t) \qquad (1.1)$$

can indicate the extent of the potential excess supply of money or the potential excess demand for goods at current prices.[s]

Using the result of footnote o, substitute for $P_1 e$ in v as follows:

$$v = (K_1 - K_2) P_1 q_1^S P_2 q_2^S / (K_1 q_2^S P_2 + K_2 q_1^S P_1)/(P_1 \bar{q}_1 + P_2 \bar{q}_2)$$

$$= (K_1 - K_2) \frac{P_1 q_1^S P_2 q_2^S}{(K_1 q_2^S P_2 + K_2 q_1^S P_1)(P_1 \bar{q}_1 + P_2 \bar{q}_2)}, \qquad (ii)$$

which, for the case of $\bar{q}_i = q_i^S$,

$$= (K_1 - K_2) \frac{P_1 q_1 P_2 q_2}{K_2 (P_1 q_1)^2 + (K_1 + K_2) P_1 q_1 P_2 q_2 + K_1 (P_2 q_2)^2}.$$

As K_2 approaches zero, v approaches $P_1 q_1 /(P_1 q_1 + P_2 q_2)$, or the share of sector 1 in the price index. If both sectors of the economy grow at the same rate, no change occurs in the coefficient of ψ. If agriculture grows faster than the rest of the economy, the coefficient of ψ becomes larger.

[r]Because ψ is a function of excess aggregate demand, it is a cyclically leading indicator. It will be positive when excess aggregate demand first increases and will then be negative as excess aggregate remains at its new level. This and the implications of the relationship between ψ and excess aggregate demand for the testing of inflation equations are discussed in Chapter 4.

[s]Harberger's inflation equation indicates potential excess aggregate demand at current prices and not actual excess aggregate demand. Actual excess aggregate demand conditions are assumed not to occur in Harberger's model. That is, real income is assumed always to equal full-employment income, no more or less. Indeed, Harberger's equation indicates how much prices must adjust to clear markets and so avoid excess aggregate demand conditions. This assumption of constant full-employment may be met in an economy with inflationary expectations when prices, expected prices, and money supply all adjust together. Thus, in an economy with inflationary expectations, excess aggregate demand is not necessary for inflation. Equations (1.29) and (1.38) are extended in Chapter 3 to incorporate inflationary expectations and to allow for inflation without excess aggregate demand. However, as is indicated in Chapter 3, to the extent money supply growth deviates from the rate required to validate inflationary expectations and growth in full-employment output, excess aggregate demand conditions do occur, unless prices adjust immediately to changes in monetary policy. This assumption of immediate price clearing is implicitly maintained in the Harberger model; it is not necessary in a monetarist model of inflation, again, as discussed in Chapter 3.

Thus, Harberger's variables reflect how much of the inflation process is due to monetarist elements.[t] If price reaction coefficients differ across sectors, equations (1.29) and (1.38) state that the inflation rate varies not only with excess aggregate demand, or monetarist factors, but also with excess demand in agriculture or the rate of change in the relative price of food. For example, beginning from a position where overall excess demand and excess demand in each sector equal zero, the price level remains unchanged according to equations (1.29) and (1.38). Then, if monetary authorities increase the money supply so that there is an excess demand for goods, the price level rises. The increase in the price level varies with the amount of excess aggregate demand relative to output. Starting over again from a position of zero excess aggregate demand, structural imbalances may also provoke a spurt in prices in the short run. If $K_1 > K_2$ and if excess demand occurs in agriculture, balanced by an equal excess supply elsewhere, in the short run, the price level rises. For this to be possible, a temporary rise in the velocity of money is required. The velocity of money, in the short run, depends on the distribution of excess aggregate demand. (Eventually, as discussed in the following section, real output is affected.) The greater the value of excess demand in agriculture, relative to overall output, and the greater $K_1 - K_2$, the greater is the short-run structural inflation. Thus both aggregate demand and structural factors can influence the short-run inflation rate.

---

[t]Harberger's equation can be seen as giving the inflation rate as a function of $\dot{M}_S/M - \dot{M}_D/\dot{M} = (\dot{M}_S - \dot{M}_D/M) = (\Sigma P_i X_i)/M$. That is, for Harberger, the potential excess supply of money at current prices is determined by the rate of change in the money supply in the current and preceding periods minus the rate of change in the variables determining the demand for money in the current period. The variables that Harberger uses are included in one test of (1.38) along with ψ. So the regression performed is:

$$\frac{\dot{P}}{P} = a\,\frac{\Sigma P_i X_i}{M} + \beta\psi + u.$$

Then, in terms of equation (1.36), a measures $\left\{[K_2 + fP_1(K_1 - K_2)]M\right\}/\Sigma P_i \bar{q}_i$ and β measures $[(K_1 - K_2)P_1 e]/\Sigma P_i \bar{q}_i$. In the case when $K_1 = K_2 = K$, a equals $KM/\Sigma P_i \bar{q}_i$ and $\beta = 0$. In this case, the price reaction coefficient K indicates, according to (1.29) and (1.38), to what extent excess aggregate demand relative to output gives rise to inflation. The inflation equation (1.38) developed here is meant to be consistent with Harberger's model, when Harberger's assumptions of the continuous existence of full-employment income and the primary importance of monetary policy are maintained. Therefore, $K = V = \Sigma P_i \bar{q}_i/M$, so that $a = (\Sigma P_i \bar{q}_i/M)(M/\Sigma P_i \bar{q}_i) = 1$, and in testing (1.38) one would expect the same coefficients that Harberger finds. If Harberger's assumption that full-employment income is continuously maintained does not hold, and in the framework of sectoral imbalances and lags in price adjustment it will not, there is a simultaneous equation bias in estimating the Harberger equation with current income as an independent variable. The implications of the bias and methods of dealing with it are discussed in Chapter 4.

An ongoing long-run inflation at a constant rate is also possible, if the government fulfills inflationary expectations by expansionary monetary and fiscal policy. A spurt (or decline) in the inflation rate is then possible if structural imbalances develop. Section IV indicates, however, that structural factors alone are not likely to lead to a permanently changed inflation rate unless fiscal and monetary policies respond in the appropriate direction.

IV. The Reformulated Structuralist Model in the Long Run

Introduction

Structuralists are often remiss in not emphasizing the importance of aggregate demand, even in structural inflation. Section IV.A. shows that unless there is a reaction on the part of monetary and fiscal authorities, inflation deriving from structural imbalances will be short-lived. Section IV.B. discusses why monetary and fiscal authorities may respond to structural inflation by raising aggregate demand. Section IV.C. contrasts the structuralist and monetarist views on the impact of aggregate demand.

IV.A.   The Impact of Structural Inflation Without Aggregate Demand Increases

Structural inflation of the sort described above can only be a short-run phenomenon, unless monetary and fiscal authorities ratify the inflation by increasing aggregate demand. Moreover, if monetary and fiscal authorities do not expand aggregate demand in response to structural inflation, any rise in the price level due to structural imbalances is followed by an equal price decline. In the reformulated structuralist model presented in Section III, the inflation rate grows, in the short run, because the rate of change of prices increases in the food sector where excess demand prevails, while the rate of price change in the nonfood sectors does not decrease with equivalent speed in the face of excess supply. Hence, the overall inflation rate rises. In terms of equation (1.29), if, for example, zero excess aggregate demand and zero excess demand in each sector are assumed, there is no inflation:

$$\frac{\dot{P}}{P} = K_2 \frac{\Sigma P_i X_i}{\Sigma P_i \overline{q}_i} + (K_1 - K_2) \frac{P_1 X_1}{\Sigma P_i \overline{q}_i} = 0. \tag{1.29}$$

However, with excess demand in agriculture ($P_1 X_1 > 0$), balanced by equal excess supply elsewhere $(P_2 X_2 < 0)$, prices rise. That this inflation can persist only in the short run is implied in equation (1.3) introduced in the summary of Enthoven's study:

$$X_i = f(P_1 \ldots P_n; P_1^e \ldots P_n^e; A) \tag{1.3}$$

which states that excess demand in the ith sector is a function of prices, expected prices, and A, the initial value of assets. With $P_1 X_1 > 0$ and $P_2 X_2 < 0$, short-run inflation occurs. But the inflation is self-limiting. Prices rise in the food sector and fall elsewhere, though at a slower rate. The resulting rise in the relative price of food reduces excess demand in agriculture. Hence, X_1 returns to zero, so that the factor which brought about the rise in prices no longer exists. Moreover, there is pressure for prices to fall back to their original level. This is because the rise in prices reduces the value of real balances, a component of A, and, thus, A, the value of assets. Before the structural inflation occurred, by assumption,

$$\sum_{i=1}^{n} P_i X_i$$

equalled zero. Now, with the fall in real balances caused by the rise in prices,

$$\sum_{i=1}^{n} P_i X_i$$

is negative. As a result, prices fall. This continues until the original value of real balances and of A are restored. Then,

$$\sum_{i=1}^{n} P_i X_i$$

again equals zero. The economy has returned to the price level prevailing before the structural inflation. This assumes that the money supply has not been increased and that neither changes in fiscal policy nor shifts in private consumption or investment occur which compensate for the decline in real balances. Thus, when excess aggregate demand is equal to zero, the occurrence of excess demand in agriculture leads only to a short-run rise in the price level. In a similar way, it can be shown that, if aggregate demand is expanded by government policy in such a way as to support an ongoing inflation at the expected rate, sectoral imbalances can lead to a short-run rise in that rate. However, the rise in the inflation rate leads to a decline in real balances and so again is temporary, unless government policy becomes even more expansionary.

In the version of the structuralist model outlined above, the rate of price change in each sector responds to excess demand conditions in the expected direction (although the speed of response varies). It is possible that prices and wages in the organized manufacturing sector will increase in spite of excess supply prevailing there. This is plausible if trade unions have growing strength. (It is less likely to the extent that unions are ambivalent about pushing up the rate of wage increase in the face of unemployment.) But even in this case, it is improbable that the inflation can persist. If the inflation does continue, real balances continue to fall.[u] Thus, there is downward pressure on prices in the competitive agriculture sector. Under the circumstances, prices and wages in the organized sector are rising relative to prices and wages in the competitive sector, since in competitive industries prices are falling in response to the ever declining real balances and aggregate demand. If this continues, the organized sector will decline in size and thus price increases in this sector will have diminishing impact on the overall inflation rate. So even under the assumption of rising prices in manufacturing, with declining prices elsewhere, eventually the overall inflation rate is likely to decline as the manufacturing sector decreases in size.

Hence, for structural factors to increase the long-run inflation rate, an accommodative monetary and fiscal policy is necessary, and some increase in the rate of monetary expansion is required, since it is unlikely that the velocity of circulation of money can increase without limit.

IV.B. The Potential for Endogenous Fiscal and Monetary Policy

Structuralists usually grant that growth in aggregate demand plays some part in the process of inflation. Their essential difference with Latin American monetarists is their belief that monetary and fiscal authorities are reacting to a prior price increase. Unlike in the monetarist framework, the inflation rate increases without an increase in the rate of growth of aggregate demand. Then, once the inflation rate increases due to structural factors, it is argued that monetary and fiscal authorities are disposed to raise the rate of growth of money supply to avoid disruptions to the economy. Pressures to implement more expansionary policies in the face of higher prices may come from several sources: First, the price rise leads to a decline in aggregate demand, through a fall in real balances and the consequent decline in investment and consumption.

---

[u]Desired real balances may fall as well. This leads to the theoretical possibility that an increase in the inflation rate will cause such a large increase in the expected rate of inflation and decline in desired real cash holdings that the inflation will feed on itself. This possibility is not of practical importance in moderate inflations.

The result is a higher unemployment rate. In itself, this higher unemployment is difficult for governments to tolerate since it threatens the governments' popular support, and so may lead to more expansionary policies.

Second, as a result of the decline in real balances, real interest rates rise; or, if there are interest rate controls, credit becomes less available. Banks are disrupted in their lending, businesses in their investment. The central bank may be under pressure from the private sector to prevent dislocations such as these that result from tight money.

Furthermore, if tax receipts do not equal government expenditures, the government relies on expansion in the money supply and in borrowings from the public to finance some of its purchases. A given inflation rate increase— unless it is matched by an increase in the rate of growth of money supply and debt sold to the public—decreases the government's purchasing power. Structuralists argue that public investments particularly suffer these circumstances since government spending for current operations is likely to be protected. The decline in private and public investment will lower the long-run rate of growth; and the general slowdown in business activity depresses growth in the short run. Monetary and fiscal authorities may feel that, for these reasons, they have little choice but to respond to the spurt in the inflation rate by engaging in more expansionary fiscal and monetary policy.[v] If they do respond, the rate of growth of the money supply is no longer exogenous, and the short-run spurt in the inflation rate, sparked by structuralist factors, persists in the long run.

IV.C. Comparison of the Role of Monetary and Fiscal Expansion in Structuralist and Monetarist Models

The monetarist position is that monetary and fiscal policies are active or exogenous. Clearly, the potential exists for these policies to respond to inflation; that is, the direction of causation may go from the inflation rate to the rate of expansion of money supply and debt sold to the public. The structuralist position requires as a necessary conditon that the monetary and fiscal policy implemented by the government be a passive variable. Although this is a crucial component of the structuralist theory, whether stated explicitly or left implicit, statistical tests to determine the validity of the hypothesis for Latin American inflations have not yet been performed. An important purpose of this study is

---

[v]Although structuralists do not specify whether money supply responds to unemployment, credit conditions, or decreases in real government purchasing power, it is perhaps the latter that is most in the spirit of the structuralist approach. Each of these response mechanisms implies that when a spurt in inflation is due to structuralist factors, the rate of monetary expansion increases.

to carry out such a test. To link the structuralist and monetarist positions to the possible results of this test, it can be noted that expansionary fiscal policy (whether undertaken to prevent a decline in employment or in real government purchasing power) is probably accompanied by expansionary monetary policy as well. That is, in the long run, since the velocity of money cannot increase without bound, a passive aggregate demand policy is likely to result in a passive money supply. Then, in the long run, the hypothesis, crucial to the structuralist argument, that aggregate demand is endogenous implies that money supply is endogenous.[w] On the other hand, an active or exogenous money supply would support the monetarist hypothesis.

Hence, the Sims test[29] for the presence of a passive or active money supply can be used to determine which if either of these hypotheses is tenable for the economies considered here. The test will be described and the results analyzed in Chapter 4.

V. Latin American Structuralism Compared to Cost-Push and Schultze's Structural Imbalance Inflation Theories

There are similarities among the structuralist and other nonmonetarist models of inflation, specifically cost-push and sectoral imbalance theories. Here I compare structuralism to these approaches.

V.A. Cost-Push Inflation and Latin American Structuralism

Several similarities in the structuralist and cost-push approaches can be cited. First, the situation which provokes structural inflation can also produce cost-push pressures. In the modified model of structuralism, it has been argued that trade unions and oligopolies may be slow to adjust the rate of price and wage change

---

[w]Evidence that the money supply is passive, however, is not necessarily inconsistent with other models of inflation. For example, outbreaks of cost-push inflation or shifts in the expected rate of inflation due to political developments can raise the inflation rate. In order to preserve their real purchasing power or to raise employment, the government may increase the money supply. For a concise statement of the interaction between money and wages in cost-push inflation see Sidney Weintraub, *A Theory of Monetary Policy under Wage Inflation* (Australia: University of Queensland Press, 1974). Passive money will also be found if government spending (financed by the sale of bonds to the public) raises prices and, if, in response, the central bank increases the money supply to lessen the resulting credit squeeze. Finally, for somewhat different reasons, a country with a fixed exchange rate is likely to have a passive money supply. Of the economies considered here, this applies only to Mexico.

downward in the face of excess supply. This may lead to inflation even if aggregate demand is not excessive, as long as excess demand occurs in the competitive sector and excess supply in the unionized sector. It is also possible, however, that unions and oligopolies initiate an exogenous increase in the rate of wage and price change above the market justified rate of increase. Assuming that oligopolies and/or unions are initially in equilibrium, that is, they have set wages and prices at a level to maximize their gain for a given level of market power, an exogenous outbreak of cost-push inflation requires a change in the underlying political, social, or economic realities which govern the level of market power of the oligopolies and/or unions.

In the case of structural inflation a rise in relative prices in the competitive sector is a problem because prices in other sectors, again due to imperfect competition, do not slow their rate of increase. Thus, both cost-push and structural inflation can occur if there exists an organized sector sheltered from market pressures. Furthermore, the larger and more sheltered this sector, the more likely that inflation of either variety will occur.

Second, in both cost-push and structural inflation, a change in relative prices leads to a higher price level. This is in direct opposition to the neoclassical monetarist view that increases in aggregate expenditures cause inflation.

Third, the use of classical monetary and fiscal restraint in either of these nonmonetarist kinds of inflation is costly in terms of unemployment and lowered output. The government can decrease aggregate demand, but it takes time for firms in the organized sector to lower their prices and, meanwhile, real output falls.

Fourth, both structural and cost-push factors cause short-run (and only short-run) spurts in the inflation rate. If the rate of monetary expansion is not adjusted upward in response to the higher rate of price change, unemployment increases. If it is adjusted upward, inflation persists at the new higher rate.

Finally, some structural theorists directly incorporate cost-push elements in their models. In these versions of the structuralist model, the rise in the relative price of food is seen as provoking an outbreak of cost-push pressures. This adds to the inflationary potential of excess demand conditions in agriculture. The logic of this argument is that the increase in the relative price of food significantly lowers the real income of blue-collar workers whose wages are substantially spent on food. In reaction to this, unions may demand an increase in their wages to match the increase in the price of food. That is, labor in strongly organized industries may respond to a rise in prices of important wage goods, such as food, with increased wage demands to defend their standard of living, in spite of the fact that these are not market justified and so cause excess supply conditions in these sectors. A structuralist model which includes such a "wage-price spiral" is discussed in more detail in the section which reviews the empirical literature.

The crucial difference between structural and cost-push inflation is that structural inflation does not require any increase in monopoly power, whereas cost-push inflation does. For cost-push inflation to occur, unions or oligopolies must exert their power to increase the wage rate or the profit rate in the organized sector. In structural inflation of the sort described here, there is no need for this; it is the distribution of excess demand across sectors that, at given levels of market power, influences the inflation rate.

V.B. Schultze's Theory of Structural Imbalances and Latin American Structuralism

In the Latin American structuralist framework, sectoral imbalances can lead to an increase in the inflation rate. Thus, this argument is a variant of the sectoral or demand-shift inflation theory developed most extensively by Schultze[30] to explain the inflation of the late 1950s in the United States. The structuralist model used by Schultze starts with the assumption of downwardly inflexible prices; shifts in tastes then provoke an increase in the price level. As tastes change, prices adjust but they move up more readily than down so that on average the price level increases.

> In the contemporary American economy prices and wages generally tend to be more flexible in an upward than in a downward direction. . . . In the industrial sector of the economy, and even more so in the service and related industries, prices tend to be rigid against declining demand.[31]

> Given downward rigidity of commodity and factor prices, the dynamics of shifting resource allocation involves a general price increase, even in the absence of excess aggregate demand.[32]

In the version of the structuralist theory developed here, it is not assumed that price reaction coefficients vary according to the direction of the price movement; rather, price reaction coefficients are symmetrical for upward and downward price changes but vary from one sector to the other. In Schultze's model, excess supply does not put downward pressure on prices, but excess demand does push prices up. The sector in which the excess demand or supply occurs does not influence the inflation rate. An implication of Schultze's model is that, given the average level of unemployment across sectors (or the level of excess aggregate demand in the economy), if the variance of sectoral unemployment rates increases, so will the inflation rate.[33] The model developed here has no such implication. Rather, it implies that, given the level of excess aggregate demand, if excess demand in agriculture (or the rate of change in the relative price of food) exogenously increases, so will the inflation rate.

2

Review of Empirical Literature

Introduction

There have been a number of attempts to test empirically the economic relationships assumed by one side or the other in the monetarist/structuralist debate. Two kinds of evidence have been used. First, as has been seen, each theory imposes different restrictions on the long-run relationship between the rate of growth of real output and the rate of inflation. In the structuralists' view, curbing inflation leads to unemployment and economic stagnation. Monetarists agree that a slowing of growth is the immediate effect of an anti-inflation policy but they argue that, in the long run, neither a higher growth rate nor a higher rate of employment can be bought through higher inflation rates. Intertemporal and cross-section studies have been done to determine which set of restrictions is consistent with the historical evidence.

The other method used to verify empirically the two models has been to relate the incidence of inflation to the presence of factors which may be considered structuralist or monetarist. Several empirical studies using the latter method are reviewed in this chapter. Some of these studies use econometric techniques. Harberger, Edel, Vogel, among others, incorporate monetarist and/or nonmonetarist variables into econometric models of inflation and then test for the significance of these factors. Others, especially those focusing on structural variables, do not use statistical testing procedures. A few of these studies are also reviewed. The chapter is divided into two sections. Section I deals with those studies emphasizing the role of structuralist factors. Section II discusses studies which concentrate on the role of money, although several of these include nonmonetarist factors as well.

I. Empirical Studies of Structural Inflation

The structuralist position developed originally out of the observation of two striking empirical relationships. First, for the most part, it has been the Latin American economies with lagging agricultural development that have experienced rapid inflation. Second, in these economies, increased inflationary pressures and serious agricultural difficulties arose simultaneously in the period after the Depression and World War II. These historical relationships are often cited as evidence of the structuralist nature of inflation. For example, in explaining inflation, Maynard uses the first phenomenon to support his conclusion on the importance of excess demand conditions in agriculture.[1]

Several studies have investigated in more detail the inflationary experience of a single country in an attempt to find a positive correlation between the strength of structuralist factors and the pace of inflation. In one such study Marnie Mueller[2] examines the impact of various structuralist factors on the inflationary process in Mexico. These factors are bottlenecks in the agriculture, foreign trade, and public sectors.

The seriousness of agricultural bottlenecks is calculated by estimating the excess demand for food while those in the foreign trade sector are represented by various terms of trade measures as well as by the growth in real imports relative to growth in GNP. Finally, the two variables used to reflect the intensity of the public sector bottleneck are the public sector deficit as a percentage of gross national product and the percentage of public expenditure allocated to investment over the two decades. These are used to evaluate the hypothesis, cited by some structuralists, that the tax system in Latin America is income inelastic so that deficits and the concomitant inflationary pressures arise inevitably with economic development.

These hypotheses are tested by looking at the inflationary experience in Mexico in two periods, the decades of the 1940s and 1950s. The relationship between inflation and economic growth seems to undergo a shift over these years.

> For every year but one (1941), the last decade contains those years in which a given rate of economic growth was accompanied by a lower rate of price increase. On this evidence the decade of the fifties suffered less from structural inflation than did that of the forties.[3]

The agricultural bottleneck is less in the latter decade and, while the deficit as a percentage of gross national product did not change significantly over the two decades, public investment as a percentage of public expenditure grew in the 1950s. Since Mexico suffered more inflation during the 1940s than the 1950s these two findings can support a structuralist interpretation. On the other hand, the capacity to import and various terms of trade measures worsened over the period. Thus, the results are felt to be inconclusive, although they do support the structuralist argument based on agricultural difficulties.

In his extensive monograph, *Food Supply and Inflation in Latin America,* Matthew Edel investigates the inflationary experience in much of Latin America on a country by country basis. He first divides Latin American economies into those with "adequate" and those with "inadequate" growth in agriculture. An adequate growth rate is defined as being sufficient, given income elasticities of demand and growth in real income, to keep the relative price of food constant. On this basis, in Mexico, Brazil, and Venezuela, food production is shown to be adequate over the period 1953-1962, while in Argentina, Chile, Colombia, Peru, and Uruguay food production falls beneath the required level. He then examines the turning points in the inflationary spirals of the countries in these two groups and finds evidence supporting the structuralist model.

> Further evidence of the effects of differential supply adequacy was found by consideration of turning points in inflationary spirals. In all of the countries with inadequate expansion of agricultural production, cases were found in which food price increases had been the first indicators to begin advancing more rapidly during an acceleration of inflation, or had served to disrupt stabilization programs. Cases included Uruguay's accelerations in 1957, 1963, and 1967; and the Argentine failure of stabilization in 1962 and those in Chile in 1957 and 1959, and Colombia in 1962. On the other hand, in the countries with adequately expanding production, this pattern did not prevail. To be sure, in 1952-1953, food prices and imports had undermined a Mexican stabilization attempt. But further expansion of Mexican production allowed a successful stabilization in 1957, and the price level has expanded only slowly since then. In Brazil, adequate expansion of food supply did not prevent inflation from accelerating in the face of declining export earnings, and severe government deficits in the 1950's, or again following the political crisis of the early 1960's. Food prices, significantly, did not lead other indicators in these episodes, which come the closest of any considered to conformity with the monetarist model.[4]

However, these findings can be explained even if increases in relative food prices are not causing the upward turning points in the inflations. As discussed in Chapter 1, Section III, food prices may respond more quickly to a given level of excess demand than prices in other sectors. If this is the case when aggregate demand is increased, if all sectors are experiencing the same amount of excess demand, food prices are likely to lead price increases in other sectors. In the second group, food production is more than adequate; in this case the relative price of food is falling over time. Thus, the effect of food prices leading other prices may be offset by the decline in relative food prices. On this interpretation increases in aggregate demand may generate the pattern of changes in food prices and overall prices that Edel observes.

Edel's study also provides an econometric model of structuralism. To do this, Edel adopts Olivera's theory of structural inflation which, unlike others, is specified in a form suitable for hypothesis testing. This theory develops the inflation rate as a function of the rate of change of the relative price of food. Olivera assumes that the relative price of food increases at a percentage rate of G_p due to the structural inadequacies discussed above. Then,

$$G_F(t) = G_P(t) + G_N(t). \tag{2.1}$$

The percentage change in the absolute food price, G_F, equals G_P plus G_N, where G_N is the percentage increase in prices in the nonfood sectors, and, which is, at first, equal to zero. When the relative price of food increases at G_P percent and the absolute price at G_F, wages and prices in the nonfood sector increase in the following manner:

$$G_S(t) = (1-a)\, G_F(t-1) \tag{2.2}$$

$$G_N(t) = (1-\beta)\, G_S(t), \tag{2.3}$$

where $G_S(t)$ is the percentage increase in wages in the nonfood sector over the period t, and $G_N(t)$, the percentage increase in nonfood prices in that period. In these equations, a and β are assumed to be greater than zero and less than one. The percentage increase in wages is a function of the prior increase in food prices and the increase in nonfood prices occurs as a proportion of the increase in wages in that sector. The inflation rate resulting from the increase in the relative price of food can be found by letting $S = (1-a)(1-\beta)$. Then,

$$G_N(t) = SG_F(t-1). \tag{2.4}$$

Substituting this into (2.1),

$$G_F(t) = SG_F(t-1) + G_P(t). \tag{2.5}$$

Thus, solving this

$$G_F = [1/(1-S)]\, G_P \tag{2.6}$$

and

$$G_N = [S/(1-S)]\, G_P. \tag{2.7}$$

The overall inflation rate which is a weighted sum of G_F and G_N is a function of G_P. Edel then uses this model and regresses G_N against G_P. In doing so, he employs cross-section data from three different time periods. In each case, he regresses inflation rates against rates of change in relative food prices observed in eighteen Latin American countries. The best results were in the following regression:

$$\frac{\text{CPI (1958)}}{\text{CPI (1953)}} = a + \beta \frac{\text{PRel. (1958)}}{\text{PRel. (1953)}} + e. \tag{2.8}$$

In this equation, CPI is the consumer price index observed in the years in parentheses, and PRel. is the relative price of food. In this regression, the estimate of β was 42.8 with a t-statistic of 5.17, with $R^2 = .62$. Regressions were also performed on data from year 1953 over year 1948, 1963 over 1958, and 1967 over 1963; in no case was the estimate of β significant. The values of R^2 were all less than 0.15.[5]

These results are weak and the model itself can be criticized on several grounds. First, it is unclear why wages react only to the price increases of food, and not to the increases in prices of nonfood goods as well, or, in other words, to the expected or actual increase in the overall cost of living. Second, wages respond in a given manner, no matter what the state of labor markets. There is no role for variations in aggregate demand. Third, in the absence of continuous increases in the relative price of food, inflation decreases to zero. That is, as soon as the relative price of food stabilizes, the rate of inflation declines. This empirical implication of the model clearly does not hold in Latin America's inflations and thus suggests that the model be modified. In sum, Edel's test provides little support for the structuralist hypothesis as he specifies it. However, the specification of the model he uses is weak in several respects, and his negative findings may be due to these weaknesses.

II. Empirical Studies of Money and Inflation

Harberger uses regression analysis to compare the validity of a version of the Latin American monetarist theory and a wage-push explanation of inflation. He employs quarterly and annual aggregate and sectoral price change data from Chile over the period 1939-1958.[6]

As described in Chapter 1, Harberger first develops an equation in which the price level is a function of the current and lagged money supply, the level of real income, and the expected cost of holding cash. To test this relationship, he takes differences of this function first and arrives at the following:

$$P_t = a + by_t + cM_t + dM_{t-1} + eA_t, \tag{2.9}$$

where P_t is the percentage change of some price index expressed as a function of the percentage change of the quantity of money during the current period, M_t, and the past period, M_{t-1}, the percentage change of real income, y_t, and the percentage change of the expected cost of holding cash, A_t, where A_t is the percentage change in the consumer price index during period $(t-1)$ minus the percentage change in the price index during period $(t-2)$. A second equation that Harberger tests omits the cost of holding cash variable.

$$P_t = a' + b'y_t + c'M_t + d'M_{t-1}. \tag{2.10}$$

Harberger then opposes this model to an alternative essentially cost-push theory of inflation. Specifically he tests the hypothesis that a special interest group, the white-collar workers, influences the general level of wages and prices through the group's influence on the legislatively determined minimum salary, the *sueldo vital*. The *sueldo vital* is set by the government, usually during the first quarter of each year, to indicate the legal minimum salary level of white-collar workers. The level of the *sueldo vital* is adjusted in part to compensate for cost-of-living changes over the past year, but it is also affected by the political strength of the white-collar lobby. Market wages are often expressed in terms of the *sueldo vital*. Thus a secretary may expect to earn one to two *sueldos vitales* a month while a middle-level executive may obtain five. When the *sueldo vital* is revalued each year, employees throughout the private sector are likely to receive salary increases. As wages are pushed up, prices also can be expected to increase. If the wage demands of white-collar workers exceed the level justified by market conditions, they may lead to a wage-push inflation. Harberger notes that, for the period he is examining, increase in the *sueldo vital* were followed by increases in wage contracts in the industrial sector of at least the same amount. But this does not indicate that these wages would not also have increased in the absence of the increase in the minimum salary. Harberger anticipates that if, in fact, the *sueldo vital* is responsible for wage-push inflation, this variable should increase the explanatory power of the rate of price change equation. To test this, Harberger presents a third equation which includes the *sueldo vital* variable.

$$P_t = a'' + b''y_t + c''M_t + d''M_{t-1} + e''A_t + f''W_t. \tag{2.11}$$

The results of Harberger's regressions, using the annual percentage rate of change [calculated from December of year $(t-1)$ to December of year (t)] in the consumer price index as the dependent variable, follow (standard errors appear in parentheses):

$$P_t = -1.05 \quad - \quad 1.05\,Y_t \; + \; 0.80\,M_t \; + \; 0.34\,M_{t-1}$$

$$(7.13) \quad\quad (0.31) \quad\quad (0.17) \quad\quad (0.16) \quad\quad\quad R^2 = 0.84$$

$$\tag{2.12}$$

$$P_t = -0.32 \quad - \quad 0.91\,Y_t \; + \; 0.74\,M_t \; + \; 0.34\,M_{t-1} \; + \; 0.20\,A_t$$

$$(0.23) \quad\quad (0.31) \quad\quad (0.16) \quad\quad (0.15) \quad\quad\quad (0.12)$$

$$R^2 = 0.87$$

$$\tag{2.13}$$

$$P_t = -1.15 - 0.89\,Y_t + 0.70\,M_t + 0.29\,M_{t-1} + 0.16\,A_t$$
$$\quad\;\; (9.56) \quad (0.32) \qquad (0.18) \qquad (0.18) \qquad\;\;\; (0.14)$$

$$+\; 0.13\,W_t$$
$$\;\;\;\,(0.22) \qquad\qquad\qquad\qquad\qquad\qquad R^2 = 0.87^7$$

$$(2.14)$$

The results indicate:

1. If real income and the money stock remain constant, the price level would also remain constant (since the constant terms are not significantly different from zero).
2. A decline in the rate of change of real income *ceteris paribus* leads to a proportionate rise in the rate of price change (since the coefficients of income do not significantly differ from one).
3. An increase in the rate of monetary expansion suggests an equal increase in the inflation rate.[a]
4. The variable constructed to measure the cost of holding money is only significant (at the ten percent level) where the *sueldo vital* variable is omitted and is not significant when the latter is included.
5. The *sueldo vital* does not appear to have a separate impact on the rate of price change.

These results are substantially confirmed when the regressions are done on quarterly data.

$$P'_t = S'_t - 0.63\,Y'_t + 0.32\,M'_t + 0.27\,D'_t$$
$$\qquad\qquad (0.22) \qquad (0.09) \qquad (0.10) \qquad\qquad R^2 = 0.52$$

$$(2.15)$$

$$P'_t = S'_t - 0.49\,Y'_t + 0.33\,M'_t + 0.26\,D'_t + 0.05\,A'_t$$
$$\qquad\qquad (0.24) \qquad (0.09) \qquad (0.10) \qquad (0.03) \qquad R^2 = 0.54$$

$$(2.16)$$

---

[a]Harberger suggests that this is so since the sum of the coefficients of the monetary variables does not significantly differ from one. However, the evidence that Harberger presents is not sufficient to prove this point. To know whether the sum of the two coefficients significantly differs from one, it is necessary to know not only the standard error of the two coefficients but also their covariance. The appropriate test performed in Chapter 4, confirms this result.

$$P'_t = S'_t - 0.49\,Y'_t + 0.31\,M'_t + 0.21\,D'_t + 0.04\,A'_t + 0.04\,W'_t$$

$$\quad\quad\quad\quad (0.24)\quad\quad (0.10)\quad\quad (0.13)\quad\quad (0.03)\quad\quad (0.06)$$

$$R^2 = 0.54^8$$

$$(2.17)$$

Here P'_t equals the percentage change in price level within each quarter; Y'_t equals the percentage change in real income from the previous to the current quarter; M'_t equals the percentage change in the money supply in the six months ending with the end of quarter t; D'_t equals a distributed-lag weighted average of the three past values of M'_t; A'_t equals the percentage change in the general price level in the year ending at the beginning of the current quarter minus percentage change in the general price level in the year before that; W'_t equals the percentage change in the *sueldo vital* at its most recent annual adjustment; and S'_t equals a seasonal constant. The results differ from those of the regressions done on annual data only in one respect. While the coefficients of Y'_t are negative, they are here significantly smaller than unity.[b] The regressions are also done on the components of the consumer price index: food prices, clothing prices, house rents, and miscellaneous prices both on annual and quarterly data. The results of these regressions are again broadly similar. The coefficients of at least one of the monetary variables is significant in the regression of each of the components, and the coefficient of the *sueldo vital* is not.

Harberger then runs further regressions on annual data using first the rate of change of the wholesale price index and then the components of the wholesale price index as dependent variables. The regression results, employing the annual percentage change in the wholesale price index as the dependent variable, follow:

$$P_{wt} = -2.30 - 0.85\,Y_t + 0.79\,M_t + 0.37\,M_{t-1}$$

$$\quad\quad (10.83)\ (0.47)\quad\quad (0.25)\quad\quad (0.24)\quad\quad\quad R^2 = 0.68$$

$$(2.18)$$

---

[b] The sum of the coefficients of $M'_t + D'_t$ does not significantly differ from 0.5, which confirms the annual results, since M'_t and D'_t refer to the six-month percentage change in the money supply, while P'_t refers to the percentage change in the price level in each quarter. Since Y'_t refers to the percentage change in real income in each quarter, to confirm the annual results, the coefficient of this variable should not differ from one.

$$P_{wt} = -1.62 - 0.72\,Y_t + 0.73\,M_t + 0.37\,M_{t-1} - 0.19\,A_t$$

$$\quad\;\;(14.79)\;\;(0.49)\qquad(0.26)\qquad(0.24)\qquad\quad(0.19)$$

$$R^2 = 0.70$$

$$(2.19)$$

$$P_{wt} = -6.64 - 0.59\,Y_t + 0.47\,M_t + 0.06\,M_{t-1} - 0.04\,A_t$$

$$\quad\;\;(12.78)\;\;(0.42)\qquad(0.24)\qquad(0.24)\qquad\quad(0.19)$$

$$+\;0.77\,W_t$$

$$\quad(0.30)\qquad\qquad\qquad\qquad\qquad R^2 = 0.80^9$$

$$(2.20)$$

These results differ from those cited above in that the *sueldo vital* is significant
and the lagged rate of change in the money stock is not. Harberger explains
these results by disaggregating the wholesale price index and running regressions
on its component parts:

$$P_{it} = -7.06 - 0.61\,Y_t + 0.16\,M_t + 0.37\,M_{t-1} - 0.21\,A_t$$

$$\quad\;\;(24.48)\;\;(0.81)\qquad(0.47)\qquad(0.46)\qquad\quad(0.35)$$

$$+\;0.90\,W_t$$

$$\quad(0.57)\qquad\qquad\qquad\qquad\qquad R^2 = 0.54$$

$$(2.21)$$

$$P_{dt} = -6.56 - 0.45\,Y_t + 0.65\,M_t + 0.02\,M_{t-1} + 0.06\,A_t$$

$$\quad\;\;(14.00)\;\;(0.46)\qquad(0.27)\qquad(0.26)\qquad\quad(0.20)$$

$$+\;0.57\,W_t$$

$$\quad(0.33)\qquad\qquad\qquad\qquad\qquad R^2 = 0.75$$

$$(2.22)$$

$$P_{Mt} = -10.54 - 0.46\,Y_t + 0.68\,M_t + 0.06\,M_{t-1} + 0.05\,A_t$$
$$(16.28)\quad (0.54)\quad\quad (0.31)\quad\quad (0.30)\quad\quad\quad (0.24)$$
$$+\ 0.66\,W_t$$
$$(0.38)\qquad\qquad\qquad\qquad\qquad\qquad R^2 = 0.72$$

$$(2.23)$$

$$P_{ft} = -2.81 - 0.20\,Y_t + 0.63\,M_t - 0.09\,M_{t-1} + 0.21\,A_t$$
$$(18.31)\quad (0.60)\quad\quad (0.35)\quad\quad (0.34)\quad\quad\quad (0.27)$$
$$+\ 0.52\,W_t$$
$$(0.43)\qquad\qquad\qquad\qquad\qquad\qquad R^2 = 0.61\,[10]$$

$$(2.24)$$

where P_{it} represents the percentage of the annual rate of change in the index of imported goods prices, and P_{dt}, that of domestic goods prices. The latter is disaggregated into rate of change of the index of food prices, P_{ft} and industrial goods prices, P_{Mt}. These regressions show that the significance of the wage variable in the wholesale price regression follows from its significance in the industrial and imported goods price regressions. Harberger feels that the significance of the *sueldo vital* in the latter equation derives from the practice of government officials of timing devaluations to coincide with increases in the *sueldo vital* to minimize the impact of the devaluation on real wages. The *sueldo vital* cannot be said to have led to the higher imported goods prices. Only in the industrial price regression can the significance of the coefficient of the *sueldo vital* be due to the existence of wage-push pressure. And here, Harberger comments that, given the oligopolistic nature of Chilean industry, "there is the possibility that industrial firms used the rise in the *sueldo vital* as a propitious excuse for making price changes they might have made in any case."[11] However, he hypothesizes that any separate influence of wages may be hidden because, when the government raises the minimum salary, it also raises the money supply to "finance" the wage rise.[12] If the money supply were not increased, the change in the minimum salary would be more significant in explaining inflation. But the money supply increase itself is sufficient to cause the higher inflation even though it is only an indirect cause in this formulation; and once it occurs the increase in the minimum salary adds nothing to the explanatory power of the inflation equation.

As evidence of this, Harberger cites the high simple correlation, 0.66, between changes in the minimum salary, generally announced in the first quarter of the year, and changes in the money supply over the course of the year. Since wages are correlated with past money supply changes, also with a correlation coefficient of 0.66, he concludes that wages react to monetary expansion in the previous period and induce monetary expansion in the subsequent period.[13]

Other studies have used the Harberger model with results generally confirming the findings of Harberger's original work. Several quantity theory based inflation equations have been estimated for Argentina.

For example, Maynard and Rijckeghem use a Harberger-type equation in their analysis of the impact of stabilization policy in Argentina.[14] Employing annual data for 1951-1964, they regress the inflation rate against the percentage change in the money supply, a dummy variable to indicate the presence of price controls, and the percentage change in negotiated wages. All variables have the expected signs; all but the last are significant.

Adolfo Cesar Diz also develops a quantity theory based inflation equation as part of a study of the demand for money in Argentina.[15] He uses quarterly observations for 1935-1962, with all variables expressed as first differences of logarithms. His dependent variables are the cost of living and wholesale price indices. His independent variables are real income, the official peso/dollar exchange rate, current and lagged money supply (defined with and without time deposits) and a variable indicating price expectations. This latter term is created by regressing changes in the rate of price change against rates of change of current and past money supply and current and past exchange rate variables. The error term of this equation is then viewed as a measure of the exogenous changes in price expectations and is included as an independent variable in the inflation equation.

The results, with the cost of living index as dependent variable and with money defined as M_1 and a coefficient of price expectations equal to 0.1, follow:

$$\dot{P} = 0.487\dot{M}_t + 0.062\dot{M}_{t-2} + 0.298\dot{M}_{t-4} + 0.043\dot{M}_{t-6}$$
$$\quad (0.074) \qquad (0.079) \qquad\quad (0.078) \qquad\quad (0.068)$$

$$+ 3.194RE - 0.550\dot{Y} + 0.101\dot{X}$$
$$\quad (0.938) \qquad (0.173) \qquad (0.023)$$

$$+ 0.027S_1 + 0.024S_2 + 0.027S_3$$
$$\quad (0.015) \qquad (0.012) \qquad (0.009)$$

$$R^2 = 0.685\text{[16]}$$

$$(2.25)$$

where $\dot{P}$ = Quarterly rate of change of the average consumer price index i from quarter $t - 1$ to quarter t.

$\dot{M}$ = Semiannual rate of change of average stock of money j from quarter $t - k - 2$ to quarter $t - k$, for $k = 0, 2, 4$, and 6.

RE = "Exogenous" changes in price expectations from quarter $t - 2$ to quarter $t - 1$.

$\dot{Y}$ = Quarterly rate of change of average real income from quarter $t - 1$ to quarter t.

$\dot{X}$ = Quarterly rate of change of official exchange rate for the U.S. dollar from the middle of quarter $t - 1$ to the middle of quarter t.

$\dot{W}$ = Quarterly rate of change of an index of nominal wages from the middle of quarter $t - 1$ to the middle of quarter t.

For the shorter period 1946-1962, wage data exists. Thus, the equation is reestimated including as an independent variable $\dot{W}$, the quarterly rate of change of an index of nominal wages, with the following results:

$$\dot{P} = 0.307\dot{M}_t + 0.153\dot{M}_{t-2} + 0.090\dot{M}_{t-4} - 0.109\dot{M}_{t-6}$$
$$(0.120) \qquad (0.123) \qquad (0.118) \qquad (0.105)$$

$$+ 3.398RE - 0.731\dot{Y} + 0.076\dot{X} + 0.074\dot{W}$$
$$(1.229) \qquad (0.264) \qquad (0.027) \qquad (0.049)$$

$$- 0.014S_1 + 0.043S_2 + 0.011S_3$$
$$(0.025) \qquad (0.022) \qquad (0.014)$$

$$R^2 = 0.679[17]$$

$$(2.26)$$

In these equations and in others that Diz estimates, with the wholesale price index as dependent variable and with M_2 substituted for M_1 and alternative coefficients of price expectations, the results are substantially the same. The coefficient of at least one money supply term is always significant. The income coefficient is always significant and negative. The coefficients of the exchange rate and the price expectation terms are again significant and positive in all equations. Finally, the coefficients of the nominal wage variable in equations estimated for 1946-1962 are insignificant in each case. Harberger's finding of little evidence for wage inflation in Chile is thus duplicated in these results for Argentina. (As Diz notes, this does not rule out the indirect impact of wages on price through

monetary authorities' accommodation of wage changes which Harberger suggests
may occur.) In sum, Diz's results offer additional evidence for an essentially
monetarist inflation process.

In yet another study of inflation in Argentina, Carlos Diaz-Alejandro uses
semiannual data for 1950-1965.[18] He regresses five different price indices
against dependent variables similar to those Diz uses.[c] He labels these as
follows: current and past money supply (X_6), hourly money wages (X_{10}), the
exchange rate (X_9), and real gross product plus imports (X_8). All variables are
expressed in percentage rates of change. Although these equations are not
essentially different from the one Diz estimates, the results differ, as the following equation illustrates ($\dot{P}$ indicates the rate of change in the cost of living index):

$$\dot{P} = -4.95 \quad + 0.06(X_6)_t \quad + 0.22(X_6)_{t-1} \quad - 0.26(X_6)_{t-2}$$
$$(3.01) \qquad (0.24) \qquad\quad (0.23) \qquad\qquad (0.22)$$

$$- 0.18(X_8)_t \quad + 0.17(X_9)_t \quad + 0.50(X_{10})_t \quad + 0.53(X_{10})_{t-1}$$
$$(0.19) \qquad\quad (0.06) \qquad\quad (0.15) \qquad\qquad (0.14)$$

$$+ 0.17(X_{10})_{t-2}$$
$$(0.14)$$

$$R^2 = 0.81$$
$$D.W. = 1.66^{[19]}$$

$$(2.27)$$

The coefficient of the real income variable is negative and significant and the
coefficient of the exchange rate is positive and significant, as in Diz's results.
However, Diz does not find the coefficient of the wage term significant; yet in
Diaz-Alejandro's equations, the wage coefficients are significant with the
expected positive sign. Using other price indices as dependent variables does not
change these results. Further, unlike Diz's results, Diaz-Alejandro's equations
indicate that no coefficient of a money supply term is significant at the five
percent level in this equation nor in other equations tested (although several
money supply coefficients are significant at the ten percent level in his other
equations). From this Diaz-Alejandro concludes that:

---

[c]Diz's data differ from those of Diaz-Alejandro in several respects. Most importantly,
Diz uses the quarterly rate of change of a quarterly index of nominal wages, while Diaz-
Alejandro uses the rate of change of quarterly averages of monthly indices of nominal
wages.

on the whole cost-push elements (wage increases and devaluations) have played an active role in the inflationary process, with monetary expansion taking a more passive role. Rather than attempting to offset price increases arising from devaluations and across-the-board wage increases by keeping the lid on money, the authorities preferred, as a rule, to validate higher money wages and prices with permissive (and at times overpermissive) increases in credit and money.[20]

Finally, Vogel[21] provides a comprehensive study of inflation in Latin America. He estimates Harberger's basic equation using combined cross-section and annual time series data for sixteen Latin American countries for 1950-1969. He also estimates equations for each country. The results, using the pooled data, follow (with t statistics in brackets):

$$P'_t = - \quad 0.031 + 0.586M'_t - 0.407M'_{t-1} - 0.298Y'_t$$
$$\quad\quad\quad\quad\quad\quad\quad [17.0] \quad\quad [11.1] \quad\quad\quad\quad [3.1]$$

$$+ \quad 0.014(\dot{P}_{t-1} - \dot{P}_{t-2})$$
$$[0.4]$$

$$\bar{R}^2 = 0.82^{22}$$
$$\text{D.W.} = 1.55$$

$$(2.28)$$

where P'_t indicates the annual rate of change in the CPI; M'_t and M'_{t-1}, respectively, the current and lagged years' rates of change in the money supply; Y'_t, the annual rate of change in real income, and $P'_{t-1} - P'_{t-2}$, with Harberger's A term used to indicate the main variable affecting the expected cost of holding cash.

As in Harberger's results: the coefficients of the current and lagged money supply variables are significant and positive; the coefficient of the price expectation term is not significant; and the real income variable's coefficient, although small, is significant and positive. Thus, Vogel's results for sixteen Latin American countries, along with the results of the Diz and the Maynard and Rijckeghem studies, substantially confirm Harberger's findings for the Chilean economy and support a monetarist view of inflation. Diaz-Alejandro's results also offer some support for the quantity theory approach in that money supply coefficients in his equations are often significant at the ten percent level. On the other hand, a significant and positive coefficient for wages is found only in the Diaz-Alejandro study.

Several comments can be made about the use of these quantity theory oriented equations to test for the basic sources of inflationary pressures in Latin America.

First, generally, they attempt to test only for the role of monetarist and wage-push factors in inflation. For the most part, they do not attempt to test for inflationary pressures arising from structuralist sources.[d] In terms of the monetarist-structuralist debate, Vogel, for example, concludes that because of the omission of structuralist variables his study can give only indirect evidence for the greater importance of monetarist factors.[23]

Second, from the results of these studies, it is not clear, what determines the money supply. Harberger raises the possibility in his original study that the rate of growth of the money supply in Chile is not exogenous but rather is dependent on the level of the *sueldo vital*. If so, this has an important implication for the interpretation of the results of estimating inflation equations with money supply terms as independent variables.

If the money supply is endogenous through government ratification of either minimum wage increases or of price increases, including it as an independent variable yields simultaneous equations bias. That is, the success in linking prices to money supply in all of these studies, except that of Diaz-Alejandro, is also consistent with the hypothesis of some structuralists that money supply is responding to prior price increases.[24] In Chapter 4, the Sims[25] procedure is used on data from several Latin American countries to test whether the money supply is an exogenous or endogenous variable in these economies.

Third, these studies consider real income as an exogenous variable. Alternative specifications of the Latin American monetarist model are possible in which real income is endogenous, as discussed in Chapter 3. Here it can be noted that if inflation and real income are simultaneously determined, the real income term in the Harberger equation may appear significant even in the absence of a neoclassical, demand-pull inflation. For example, if an exogenous rise in prices occurs due to structuralist factors, real balances decline. As a result of the decline in the real balance component of wealth, aggregate demand and real income are likely to fall. Thus, a negative correlation between real income and the inflation rate may be found if inflation is determined by monetarist or structuralist factors.

Fourth, several of these studies test for the existence of a nonmonetarist source of inflation by including a measure of wage changes as an independent

[d]Diaz-Alejandro does include the percentage change in the exchange rate. The significant coefficient found indicates the possibility of an independent impact of the exchange rate on inflation. However, one would expect the coefficient of this variable to be significant even in a pure monetarist inflation, since inflation is likely to affect the exchange rate.

variable. It is argued that a significant coefficient on the wage variable will indicate the presence of wage-push inflationary pressures. While structuralist and wage-push pressures alike are nonmonetarist causes of inflation, structuralist inflation, as discussed above, can occur with or without cost-push inflation. Although structuralist pressures on the rate of price change may be magnified through cost-push pressures, this possibility is not relied upon here in the derivation of a structuralist model and, from the evidence of these studies, probably should not be. In the equations estimated with a wage term as an independent variable, the coefficients of the wage terms are consistently significant only in Diaz-Alejandro's study, using Argentinian data. Moreover, there are several reasons why such a term may appear to be significant even though there is no autonomous pressure on the price level from wages. First, wages may move with prices because they are influenced by prices. Thus, wage changes will be correlated with price changes although causality is not established. Second, there is a problem of multicollinearity. Wages and prices may be influenced by the same factors. More specifically, wages may reflect the state of excess aggregate demand in the labor market and thus may be a proxy for demand-pull pressures. This possibility is examined in an article by Ronald Koot.[26]

To summarize Koot's argument: Assume that an administered wage, such as the *sueldo vital* in Chile, responds in part to market conditions. That is, if the equilibrium level of wages for white-collar workers increases due to a shift in demand for these workers, the authorities respond by adjusting the *sueldo vital* to equate demand and supply and prevent a shortage of this kind of labor. In times of high aggregate demand, this labor market tightens, and the governmental authorities respond by increasing the *sueldo vital*, since they take into account labor market conditions in their determination of the appropriate level of this wage. Also, in general, wages increase in response to the high aggregate demand and tightening of labor markets. The *sueldo vital* and average wages will be correlated and it may be concluded that the higher *sueldo vital* pushed up wages when it is rather the state of the labor market which is responsible for the increasing rate of wage change. This argument will hold, a fortiori, if market determined rather than administratively determined wages are included in an inflation equation, as is true in the Diaz-Alejandro study, for example.

Koot attempts to formulate a wage change variable which is free from this problem and which will measure only the autonomous pressures on wages; that is, those not related to increases in aggregate demand. However, his is not an adequate test for the presence of cost-push inflation either.

To derive an estimate of the autonomous rate of change of wages, Koot first develops the following wage equation to explain the total rate of change of wages:

$$W^T = a + bU^{-1} + cC_{-1} + dT + e, \tag{2.29}$$

Where W^T is the total rate of change of industrial money wages; U^{-1} is the inverse of the unemployment rate and is included as a proxy variable for the excess demand for labor; C_{-1} is the rate of change of the consumer price index with a one year lag; and T is the percentage of the total labor force having union membership, which serves as a measure of union strength.

Koot hypothesizes that the rate of change of money wages in a completely competitive market would be a function of excess demand conditions (represented by U^{-1}) alone. He then estimates Harberger inflation equations, using the remaining "autonomous" wage change factors, W^A, in place of the *sueldo vital*, where

$$W^A = cC_{-1} + dT + e. \tag{2.30}$$

Thus, W^A includes lagged consumer prices as one of its elements. This variable's coefficient is significant in the equation Koot estimates with the rate of change in the wholesale price index as dependent variable. However, as constructed, the autonomous wage variable is a linear combination not only of a measure of unionization but also of lagged price changes and an error term. If parties to wage agreements, even in nonunion firms, form contracts that will hold over a period of time, their expectation of the course prices will take over that period should influence the level of the wage they settle on. Their expectations as to the future rate of price change are likely to be formed as a function of past price changes. Thus, in the wholesale industrial price equation, the significance of the W^A variable, which includes lagged price changes, may reflect the influence of price expectations and cannot be considered to represent only autonomous pressures on wages, as desired. Hence, there are problems in testing for wage-push inflation by including either wage changes or Koot's autonomous wage term independent variable in an inflation equation.

In summary, these empirical studies generally establish a strong relationship between money and inflation. However, they do not test for reverse direction of causality; nor do they directly test for a nonmonetarist source of inflation based on structural pressures from the agricultural sector.

3
Alternative Demand-Pull Approaches and Testable Implications of the Structuralist and Monetarist Models

Introduction

This chapter develops a broad-based model of the Latin American monetarist or demand-pull theory of inflation and integrates the reformulated structuralist model into this approach. The neoclassical demand-pull model derived here can serve as an alternative to the Harberger quantity theory equation to measure monetarist inflationary pressures. It differs from the Harberger model, primarily, in its emphasis on the short-run rather than the long-run determination of income and inflation. Unlike in the quantity theory model, actual real income need not always be at the full-employment level. In the framework of this model, structural imbalances will be seen to have a short-run impact on the unemployment rate and on the real income level as well as on the inflation rate.

Although there is no single Latin American monetarist model, the theory is sufficiently detailed to develop a relatively rigorous formulation of the hypothesis. The bases of the model derived in this chapter are two equations: one describes the rate of inflation and the other the level of real income or the unemployment rate. Stress is placed on the inflation equation which can be used alone in a Phillips-curve type model of the Latin American monetarist hypothesis.

In Section I, an IS-LM analysis is used to derive a broad-based demand-pull model of inflation and to compare this to the Harberger quantity theory of inflation described in Chapter 1. Section II integrates the reformulated Latin American structuralist hypothesis into the model of Section I. Section III discusses the testable implications of the Latin American monetarist and structuralist hypotheses.

I. The Phillips-Curve Approach to Measuring Excess Aggregate Demand

Introduction

Sections I.A and I.B derive a demand-pull inflation model based on the IS-LM approach and compare this to the Harberger model. In Section I.A the static IS-LM framework is developed. In Section I.B this framework is extended to generate a Phillips-curve type of inflation equation. One problem which arises in estimating the Phillips curve is the creation of a variable to represent the unobservable inflationary expectations term. This is examined in Section I.C. Section I.D then discusses the use of the Phillips-curve equation to measure excess aggregate demand, or

$$\sum_{i=1}^{n} P_i X_i \ \Big/ \ \sum_{i=1}^{n} P_i \bar{q_i} \quad {}^{a}$$

in equation (1.29) and inflationary expectations, and to test the role of these factors in inflation.

I.A. The Static IS-LM Framework

The classical derivation of a monetarist inflation equation for Chile is done by Harberger.[1] As discussed above his equation is based on the quantity theory equation:

$$MV = PY. \tag{3.1}$$

Taking percentage first differences, and allowing the coefficients to differ from unity, results in:

$$\frac{\dot{P}}{P} = a + a_1 \frac{\dot{M}}{M} + a_2 \frac{\dot{V}}{V} + a_3 \frac{\dot{Y}}{Y} \qquad a_1 > 0 \qquad a_2 > 0 \qquad a_3 < 0. \tag{3.2}$$

In estimating (3.2), for reasons outlined above, Harberger replaces the change in velocity variable with the second difference of the price series, so that this latter variable is used as a measure of the cost of holding money.

Although (3.2) is often used as the specification of the neoclassical price model in the literature on Latin American inflation, alternative forms are possible.[2] More specifically, two assumptions that the quantity theory inflation equation embodies are not necessary to the Latin American monetarist view of inflation. These are: first, that fiscal policy does not have an impact on inflation; and second, that prices are sufficiently flexible so that real income does not differ

---

[a]Hereafter the range of the index on this term is suppressed. It should be assumed that all summations are over the range 1 to n as indicated here.

from its full-employment level. The more general demand-pull model differs from the quantity theory in not maintaining these assumptions.

The first differences between the Harberger model and demand-pull explanations can be shown using a standard IS-LM framework in an economy without inflationary expectations:[3]

$$Y = h(E_o, r) \qquad h_{E_o} > 0 \qquad h_r < 0 \qquad (3.3a)$$

$$Y = g(M_o, P, r) \qquad g_{M_o} > 0 \qquad g_P < 0 \qquad g_r > 0 \quad (3.3b)$$

$$Y = Y_f, \qquad (3.3c)$$

where h is the IS function, g is the LM function, and Y_f denotes long-run full-employment income or maximum non-inflationary output. The Y_f term is defined as occurring at the zero-inflation-unemployment rate, U_f, when there are no inflationary expectations.[4] The exogenous variables are E_o, M_o, and Y_f, the levels of real expenditures (both private and public), the money supply, and, as noted, real full-employment output, respectively. In equilibrium, when $Y = Y_f$, these three equations can be solved for the three dependent variables, real output (Y), the price level (P), and the rate of interest (r).

The reduced form equation for the price level may be written as

$$P = \theta(E_o, M_o, Y_f)$$

$$\theta_{E_o} > 0 \qquad \theta_{M_o} > 0 \qquad \theta_{Y_f} < 0. \qquad (3.4)$$

The partial derivatives indicate that prices may rise — in a demand-pull inflation — due to increases in private or governmental exogenous expenditures and/or increases in the money supply. Either of these two causes of price increases may be viewed as monetarist in the Latin American framework, whereas only the increase in the money supply is seen as a cause of inflation in the Harberger model.

To justify omitting shifts in public spending as a cause of price rises, one of several assumptions can be made. The assumption most relevant to the Latin American experience is simply that, although exogenous shifts in public or private expenditure do induce increases in the price level, they are a relatively unimportant factor (expecially in comparison to shifts in M_o) in explaining the price increases that occur. Therefore, they can be ignored without doing too much violence to the predictive power of an inflation model.[b]

---

[b]Harberger seems to rely on this justification for not including changes in government spending (or the real interest rate) in his model, although others, such as various explanations for "crowding-out," are possible.

I.B. The Phillips-Curve Equation

Although equations (3.3a) through (3.3c) can be utilized to explain the price level, the system is essentially static so that it cannot form the basis of an inflation equation. Moreover, like the Harberger equation, the resulting reduced form equation for the price level (3.4) requires actual income to be equal to full-employment income, Y_f. However, the assumption that the economy is always at full-employment income is inconsistent with the reformulated structuralist hypothesis. Instantaneous price adjustment to market clearing levels in all sectors is required for the economy to be continuously at full employment. But if prices immediately adjusted throughout the economy, there would be no observable differences in price reaction coefficients across sectors. For example, if price reaction coefficients are sufficiently large, then a good part of the price adjustment process would occur within the quarter. Then even if $K_1 > K_2$, sectoral imbalances would not have any impact on the average inflation rate over the quarter. Here the IS-LM model is extended to explain inflation in a framework which does not assume instantaneous price adjustment to market clearing levels and which allows income to deviate from its full-employment level. In doing so, the second distinction between this and the quantity theory approach becomes evident. This rests on the divergence of real income from the full-employment income level, in the short run.

The IS-LM model can be augmented to allow for inflation in the following way:

$$Y = h(E_o, r) \tag{3.3a'}$$

$$Y = g'(M_o, P, i) \qquad g_i' > 0 \tag{3.3b'}$$

$$\dot{P}/P = j'(Y_f - Y, (\dot{P}/P)^e) \qquad j'_{(Y_f - Y)} < 0, j'_{(\dot{P}/P)^e} > 0,$$

$$j'(0, (\dot{P}/P)^e) = (\dot{P}/P)^e. \tag{3.3c'}$$

Here, $\dot{P}/P$ is the percentage rate of change of prices and $(\dot{P}/P)^e$ is the expected inflation rate. The real rate of interest is identified as r, and i is the market rate of interest and, hence, the cost of holding money. The market rate of interest does not equal the real rate of interest if there is an expectation of future price changes. Rather, $i = (\dot{P}/P)^e + r$. Equation (3.3a) and (3.3a') are identical. Equation (3.3b') is now modified to allow for the fact that the demand for money depends upon the money (market) rate of interest rather than the real rate of interest.[5]

Equation (3.3c') is a Phillips-curve type of equation where the rate of change of prices is determined in part by the expected inflation rate. The inflationary

expectations term $(\dot{P}/P)^e$ enters equation (3.3c$'$) as a consequence of the
discrete nature of the price setting process and the lack of perfect information. Because changing prices is costly, for reasons discussed above, prices
will be set for some time. Then firms and individuals must guess the rate of
inflation over the time interval in which prices will be constant. (The role
of and the manner in which inflationary expectations are formed are discussed further in Section I.C below.)

Equation (3.3c$'$) also indicates that the inflation rate, given the level
of inflationary expectations, varies inversely with the GNP gap $(Y_f - Y)$ or
the unemployment rate, in the short run. Several theories have been offered
to explain the existence of a short-run Phillips curve, i.e., a negative relationship between unemployment and inflation. In one approach, the approach
adopted here, a short-run Phillips curve results when aggregate demand is
varied in an economy in which structural imbalances exist across sectors.[6]
Structural or sectoral imbalances exist because prices do not adjust instantaneously to their market-clearing levels. This assumption of sectoral imbalances due to lags in price adjustments does not lead to changing inflation
with shifts in the distribution of sectoral imbalances in this model, since it
is implicitly assumed that price reaction coefficients are the same across all
sectors.[c] Thus the model does not show how the distribution of excess demand,
among sectors with different price reaction coefficients, influence the inflation
rate, at a given level of excess aggregate demand. Rather, the focus is on the
derivation of a Phillips curve.[7]

Movement along a short-run Phillips curve occurs when changes in monetary and fiscal policy shift the economy from an equilibrium inflation rate.
An equilibrium inflation rate results if monetary authorities increase the money
supply at a rate equal to the sum of the rates of change in real income, in
velocity (both assumed known and exogenous), and in the expected price level.
Inflationary expectations are unchanged and an equilibrium inflation rate prevails. Aggregate demand equals aggregate supply and actual income, Y, equals
full-employment income Y_f. Prices in those sectors which are in equilibrium
rise at the overall expected inflation rate. Although excess aggregate demand is
zero, some sectors experience excess demand while other sectors experience
excess supply. The rate of price change is less than the expected inflation rate
in the excess supply markets and greater than this rate in the excess demand
markets so that overall inflation proceeds at the expected rate. Unemployment
exists in the excess supply sectors and vacancies exist in the excess demand
sectors; the real wage needs to fall in the excess supply sectors and to rise in the
excess demand sectors to equilibrate demand and supply for labor in each

---

[c]It will be shown that shifts in the distribution of sectoral imbalances will cause the
short-run Phillips curve to shift when price reaction coefficients are allowed to vary across
sectors.

market. Eventually markets clear. Exogenous shifts in supply and demand, however, are always occurring in the economy. Thus, in the absence of instantaneously adjusting prices and wages, there will always be some sectors with unemployment and others with vacancies.

The unemployment that results when excess demand in some sectors balances excess supply in others so that the overall inflation rate continues at its expected level has been termed the natural rate of unemployment. It has also been termed the non-inflationary rate of unemployment since with zero inflationary expectations, this rate implies a zero inflation rate. This unemployment rate, here labelled U_f, is not zero. U_f includes, as indicated, frictional unemployment which occurs when vacancies in some sectors balance unemployment in others. It also includes structural unemployment which occurs when a worker's productivity and, hence, the wage offered to him by an employer, is lower than the wage at which he wishes to work, or, in the presence of minimum wage laws, can work.

To show how a Phillips curve is derived in the framework of sectoral imbalances, assume, to begin with, that the economy is at U_f with zero inflationary expectations, and, therefore, zero inflation. The economy is operating at the point a at which the Phillips curve denoted PP' in Figure 3-1 goes through U_f with a zero inflation rate. If monetary and fiscal authorities expand

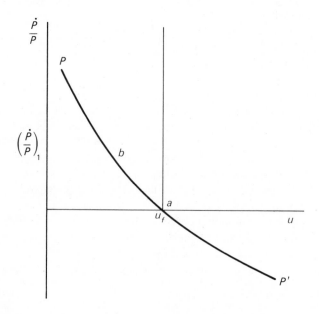

Figure 3-1. The Phillips Curve with Zero Inflationary Expectations

aggregate demand, sectors with vacancies as well as sectors with unemployment experience an increase in demand. Thus, the price rise accelerates in the excess demand sectors and the price decline slows in the excess supply sectors, so that the overall price level now rises. Furthermore, the sectors with unemployment respond to the increase in demand by increasing output and employment. The increased aggregate demand has resulted in a rise in prices and, in the short run, in a decline in unemployment as well. A movement along a short-run Phillips curve results.[8] For example, on PP' in Figure 3-1, there is a movement from point a to point b where unemployment is below U_f and the actual inflation rate $(\dot{P}/P_1)$ is greater than the anticipated zero rate of inflation. Thus, as indicated by equation (3.3c), with inflationary expectations equal to zero, the inflation rate is positive when output Y is greater than equilibrium full-employment output Y_f.

But the Phillips curve is unstable. Inflationary expectations as well as unemployment (or a GNP gap) enter into equation (3.3c). The inflation which occurs at point a eventually provokes inflationary expectations. When this occurs, prices rise at the expected inflation rate even when labor markets are in equilibrium, i.e., when $U = U_f$. That is, the Phillips curve will shift upward.[9] In sum, as equation (3.3c) states, the actual inflation rate varies with the level of excess demand observed in labor markets or goods markets, i.e., the divergence of U from U_f or Y from Y_f as well as with the expected inflation rate. It will be argued below that the actual inflation rate varies, in addition, with the distribution of sectoral imbalances. That is, once price reaction coefficients are allowed to vary across sectors, the Phillips curve shifts not only with changes in inflationary expectations but also with exogenous shifts in sectoral imbalances.[d]

Equation (3.3c') is very different from the quantity-theory price equation estimated by Harberger. The quantity-theory equation (3.1) may be viewed as a counterpart to equation (3.3b), that is, the LM curve, except that (3.3b) does not contain any measure of the potential output or the supply of goods. In the Harberger version of the quantity-theory equation, potential output is not

---

[d]As noted, Tobin makes an additional assumption in his model, not included here, that prices in all sectors move up more readily than down. This assumption of asymmetry in price reaction speeds is not necessary for the existence of structural imbalances to generate a Phillips curve when aggregate demand is varied. However, if this assumption is maintained, Y_f, as Tobin defines it, implies a positive inflation rate even in the absence of inflationary price expectations. Further, as discussed in Note 7, this assumption implies that the dispersion as well as the level of unemployment will influence the inflation rate. In the model developed here, as in the Tobin and Archibald model, the unemployment rate reflects the level of aggregate demand and helps determine the inflation rate. However, prices are not assumed to move up more readily than down; rather, prices are assumed to react at different speeds to excess demand in different sectors. Like Tobin's model, this implies that Y_f may not entail a zero inflation unemployment rate, depending on where unemployment occurs. Tobin also touches on the implication of differing price reaction coefficients in a model of sectoral imbalances. As he states, "An unlucky random drawing might put the excess demands in highly responsive markets and the excess supplies in especially unresponsive ones." See Tobin, "Inflation and Unemployment," p. 10.

omitted; that is, it is assumed that the economy is producing at its potential, $Y = Y_f$, and so equations (3.1) and (3.2) contain the supply of goods, since they contain Y. In the classical version of the quantity theory, this assumption was coupled with the notion that velocity was constant. This led to the classical conclusion that changes in the money supply were mirrored in equal percentage changes in the price level. Harberger's model does not assume that velocity is constant. However, in his model real income is assumed always to be fixed at full employment. Even in the short run, income is determined by supply. This is the second major difference between the IS-LM framework and the Harberger model. In Harberger's formulation excess aggregate demand must be measured by the underlying factors causing it, since real income remains substantially steady at the full-employment level. Therefore, no GNP gap appears to reflect, along with the expected inflation rate, the extent of demand pressures.

In the Phillips-curve model derived here, the income variable included in (3.1) and (3.2) is not exogenous. The Phillips-curve model and the Harberger model can be reconciled in the long run since in both models, in the long run, income will be at its equilibrium full-employment level. In the short run, income can be viewed as being determined simultaneously with inflation and the rate of interest in the three-equation model. This model suggests that equations (3.3a') and (3.3b') be used to determine Y and r, conditional on P, and that P be determined conditional on Y and r, simultaneously in equation (3.3c'). Thus, using the assumption that $i = r + (\dot{P}/P)^e$, the general form of the equation combining (3.3a') and (3.3b') is

$$Y = l\,[E_o, M_o, P, (\dot{P}/P)^e].\qquad\qquad(3.5)$$

Real income is determined by exogenous private and public expenditures, the money supply, the price level — which essentially acts as a deflator for E_o and M_o — and the expected rate of inflation. The partial derivative $l_{(\dot{P}/P)^e}$ is positive because an increase in the expected rate of inflation increases the cost of holding money, and, hence, increases the velocity of the money supply. This equation obviously represents only a first approximation to the determination of income and is difficult to estimate for Latin America since quarterly statistics for Y and E_o are lacking. Alternatively, a Phillips curve equation can be estimated using ordinary least squares with the existence of simultaneous equations bias recognized.

Estimating a Phillips curve may allow for a test of whether the unemployment rate does vary inversely with the inflation rate, as the above model predicts.[e] However, even though such a model may prove to be correct, this

---

[e]The problem is that the ordinary least-squares estimation of a Phillips-curve equation which results from the simultaneous determination of income or the unemployment rate and inflation may lead to an underestimation of the negative impact of unemployment on inflation.

does not invalidate the Harberger equation as a test of the ultimate factors causing changes in inflation. The Harberger model may well be quite adequate if it is assumed that money supply is exogenous and that fiscal policy has little role to play. The Harberger quantity-theory equation then acts as a reduced-form equation where the basic causes of inflation, rather than the intermediate link between these and the inflation rate, i.e., the unemployment rate or income gap, are included as independent variables.[10]

I.C. The Measurement of Inflationary Expectations

A major problem in estimating Phillips-curve equations of the equation (3.3c$'$) genre is that the expectations variable, $(\dot{P}/P)^e$, is not directly observable. Therefore, it is necessary to replace $(\dot{P}/P)^e$ with a proxy variable which is observable. Since the absence of expectational data is a problem common to almost all countries, several techniques have been adopted in the literature to deal with the problem. Perhaps the most frequently utilized assumption is that the currently expected rate of inflation is dependent on all or the most recent past rates of inflation; that is:

$$\left(\frac{\dot{P}}{P}\right)^e_t = j\left[\left(\frac{\dot{P}}{P}\right)_{t-1}, \left(\frac{\dot{P}}{P}\right)_{t-2}, \cdots \left(\frac{\dot{P}}{P}\right)_{t-n}\right]. \qquad (3.6)$$

A method of implementing equation (3.6) is to assume that the lag weights implicit in the function j, follow an a priori specified form. The simplest assumption would be that current expectations are equal to the most recent observed rate of inflation; that is:

$$\left(\frac{\dot{P}}{P}\right)^e = \left(\frac{\dot{P}}{P}\right)_{t-1}. \qquad (3.7)$$

Estimating the inflation equation (3.3c$'$), given equation (3.7) as the expectation mechanism, is equivalent to inserting a lagged dependent variable into (3.3c$'$). The econometric problems associated with this technique which, in the presence of autocorrelated residuals, include biased estimates of the coefficient, are outlined in Johnston.[11]

A variation of (3.6) is to allow the lag weights to follow a geometrically declining pattern.

$$\left(\frac{\dot{P}}{P}\right)^e_t = \lambda \sum_{i=1}^{n} \left(\frac{\dot{P}}{P}\right)_{t-i} (1 - \lambda)^i \tag{3.8}$$

where λ is a parameter which controls the speed of the geometric decline and n is the length of the lag. Although theoretically the length of the lag may be infinitely long, that is, $n = \infty$, data limitations obviously force one to choose a finite value of n. In a geometrically declining series, a relatively small value of n can be chosen where

$$\sum_{i=n+1}^{\infty} (1 - \lambda)^i$$

is small so that the bias resulting from omitting those far distant rates of inflation is also small. A common technique of estimating equation (3.3c'), given the expectational mechanism of equation (3.8), is to use a two-stage procedure. In the first stage, λ is varied between the values of zero and unity to create alternative expectational series. In the second stage, equation (3.3c') is estimated, using the created expectational series. It is assumed that the correct value of λ is the value which maximizes the R^2 of equation (3.3c'). See, for example, Cagan,[12] Solow,[13] and Deaver.[14] Clearly, there are a large number of variants on this technique.[f]

I.D. The Use of the Phillips–Curve Equation to Measure $\Sigma P_i X_i / \Sigma P_i \bar{q}_i$ and Inflationary Expectations

With zero inflationary expectations, inflation depends only on excess aggregate demand or the GNP gap $(Y_f - Y)$. When inflationary expectations exist in an economy, inflation is determined by the expected rate of price change as well as by excess aggregate demand and, thus, an inflationary expectations term must

---

[f]Recent theoretical work on the formation of rational expectations has indicated that, if all available information is used, the expected price level will be the mathematical expected value of the actual price level. Thus the expected price level will diverge from the actual price level only by a random forecasting error. However, as shown by Benjamin Friedman in "Rational Expectations are Really Adaptive After All," unpublished, Harvard, February 1975, rational expectations can be closely approximated by an adaptive expectation mechanism of the sort discussed here. This is so if individuals gradually acquire knowledge of the workings of the system using a least-squares learning technique. For further discussion of rational versus adaptive expectations see Robert J. Gordon, "Recent Developments in the Theory of Inflation and Unemployment."

be added to inflation equation (1.29) to represent monetarist pressures on prices. In the presence of inflationary expectations, this becomes:

$$\frac{\dot{P}}{P} = \frac{K_2 \Sigma P_i X_i}{\Sigma P_i \bar{q}_i} + \frac{(K_1 - K_2) P_1 X_1}{\Sigma P_i \bar{q}_i} + \gamma \left(\frac{\dot{P}}{P}\right)^e . \tag{1.29'}$$

To show the interaction of the excess aggregate demand and inflationary expectations terms in equation (1.29'), assume that the economy is in an inflationary equilibrium where $Y_f - Y$ equals zero; and all markets are in equilibrium in real terms. However, the overall price and wage rate levels are expected to rise. If prices are expected to increase, demand and supply curves over time shift upwards in each market; that is, they shift up so that actual prices rise by the expected amount as shown in the D' and S' curves in Figure 3-2. Since demand and supply curves shift together, no excess demand appears. Thus, following Tobin, the rate of change of prices or wages in a market can be divided into two components. One is identified as the equilibrium component which is equal to the expected inflation rate. The other is identified as the disequilibrium component which depends on excess demand in that market.[15] In a similar way, it is possible to divide the overall pressure on prices into these equilibrium and disequilibrium elements. The disequilibrium component of a price change varies with $\Sigma P_i X_i / \Sigma P_i \bar{q}_i$ and the distribution of excess aggregate demand. The

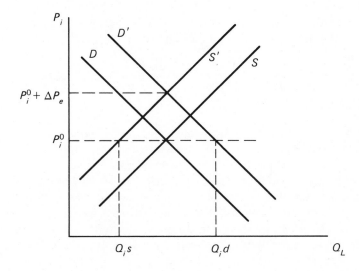

Figure 3-2. The Impact of Validated Inflationary Expectations on Sector i's Prices

equilibrium component is equivalent to $(\dot{P}/P)^e$. Then employing the Phillips-curve approach $(\dot{P}/P)^e$ reflects inflationary expectations and the GNP gap reflects $\Sigma P_i X_i / \Sigma P_i \bar{q}_i$.[g]

Excess aggregate demand and excess demand in each sector may be zero. However, inflation is still positive if $(\dot{P}/P)^e$ is. The presence of inflationary expectations alone is sufficient, in the short run, to raise prices. Assuming constant real income, if money supply expansion continues at the expected inflation rate, the unemployment rate does not fall below its full-employment level. The fact that no overall excess demand is being observed in the labor markets does not mean that prices are stable. Prices are expected to rise, and, so, do rise. Because money expansion occurs at the same rate as the expectation-caused price rise, real balances remain constant. The price rise is validated. As indicated by equation (1.3), in a market with zero X_i to begin with, $X_i = f(P_1, \ldots, P_n; P_1^e, \ldots, P_n^e; A)$ remains zero as all arguments of equation (1.3) change proportionally. Thus, there is no visible change in the goods market or labor market. The evidence for the excess supply of money is in the rising prices. Markets clear and no shortages or excess demand for labor appear or need to appear to push up prices. Income will continue at the full-employment level and inflation will continue at the equilibrium expected rate. In this case, when money supply growth ratifies inflationary expectations, the actual inflation rate is equal to the expected inflation rate.

If the rate of monetary expansion deviates from the expected inflation rate, changes in the inflation rate are the eventual result. (Although the income velocity of money may adjust to some extent). As the following section indicates, exogenous shifts in the distribution of excess aggregate demand also cause inflation to deviate from the equilibrium rate.

II. Structural Inflation in Terms of the IS-LM Framework

In the previous sections, a demand-pull model of inflation was described which may serve as an alternative to the quantity theory approach. In this model, the inflation process is viewed as depending solely on demand-pull and expectational factors. The reformulated structuralist model developed in Chapter 1, Section III and modified in Chapter 3, Section 1 led to the derivation of an inflation equation in which the distribution as well as the level of excess demand and the anticipated inflation rate affect the inflation rate. To show the impact of the distribution of aggregate demand on the inflation rate

---

[g]The variables of the quantity theory inflation equation can be seen to reflect the underlying factors that will determine both the equilibrium and disequilibrium components of the inflation rate.

in terms of the IS-LM analysis, assume that the economy is in equilibrium. There is no inflation; consequently, there are no inflationary expectations. Zero excess demand prevails in each sector ($P_i X_i = 0$, for all i). Then, an increase in the absolute price of food occurs due to excess demand in agriculture. Excess supply conditions, elsewhere in the economy, balance excess demand in agriculture. Hence, aggregate demand is still not excessive ($P_1 X_1 > 0$, and, $P_1 X_1 = -P_2 X_2$). If the downward pressure in the nonfood markets produces a fall in prices as rapidly as the upward pressure in the food market produces a rise in prices ($K_1 = K_2$), the overall price level remains unchanged. No inflation results. If the assumption of differing price reaction coefficients is added to the model, the relative price rise in agriculture can dictate a higher price level. This price increase, however, is only a short-run phenomenon. Excess supply conditions persist in the sectors with slowly adjusting prices, so that, eventually, prices do adjust downward there. Moreover, the real balance effect assures that the overall price level returns to its former state, in the long run. Because, in the short run, excess demand in agriculture and excess supply elsewhere, cause overall prices to rise; they also cause real balances to fall. With lower real money balances, the income velocity of money must increase or real income must drop. Although lower real money balances may not lead to a decline in real income at first, since velocity may rise temporarily, after some time, they are likely to have just this effect. Thus, the decline in real money balances eventually results in lower aggregate demand and a decline in real income and employment, until overall prices drop to their initial level. [Since the X_is are functions of real wealth, of which real balances are a component, the price rise results in a negative $\Sigma P_i X_i$ term in equation (1.29) until prices fall again.]

This result can be shown graphically using the IS-LM analysis. Equations 3.3a and 3.3b, respectively, the IS and LM curves, are represented in Figure 3-3, where i is the real interest rate and Y, the real income level. At the initial point of equilibrium, a, actual real income, Y, is equal to full-employment real income, Y_f. Excess demand is zero in all markets and the overall price level is constant. Then the price level rises due to excess demand in agriculture and excess supply elsewhere. This shifts the IS and LM curves back to the IS^2 and LM^2 positions,[h] due to the decline in real balances. The IS and LM curves now intersect at a point b, below full-employment income. Prices now rise at an unemployment rate which was previously consistent with a fall in prices. Essentially the structural inflation has caused a short-run adverse shift of the Phillips curve. This is shown in Figure 3-1 by a shift of the Phillips curve up from the original PP' position. Due to the increased unemployment and drop in real income, prices then decline until they return to their initial level and the IS and LM curves again intersect at Y_f and the Phillips curve returns to PP'.

---

[h]This assumes a real balance effect in the consumption sector. In the absence of this, only the LM curve shifts out and then back.

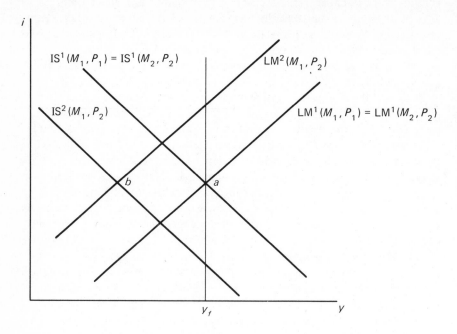

Figure 3-3. The Impact of Structural Inflation in an IS-LM Framework

Hence, maintaining the assumption of no inflationary expectations, structuralist factors lead to a short-run rise in the price level followed by a decline. The over-all price level is unaffected in the long run by institutional rigidities in agriculture. The shift in the Phillips curve is temporary.

Adding the assumption of a passive money supply changes this result. In response to the short-run price rise, the government may increase the money supply. This is done to maintain real balances and so to prevent a rise in unemployment and a decline in government and private real purchasing power. Real balances are restored ($M_1/P_1 = M_2/P_2$). In Figure 3-3, the IS and LM curves are returned to their initial IS^1 and LM^1 positions without prices falling back to their original level.

In summary, excess demand in agriculture (balanced by excess supply else-where) leads to an initial advance in the price level. An increase in the money stock follows and, as a result, the price level remains at its new higher level. A passive money supply implies that, after the initial increase in the price level, and the money stock to validate it, fiscal and monetary policy are no longer expansive. If this is the case (and maintaining the assumption of no inflationary expectations) there is no reason for any further inflation. If exogenous relative food prices increase again, however, this implies another advance in the price level which, if ratified by a rise in the money supply, becomes permanent.

Inflationary expectations so far have been assumed to be nonexistent. In an economy subject to inflation, expectations of further price rises are likely to develop. A self-generating inflation results if price rises are ratified by an increase in money aggregate demand so that inflationary expectations are fulfilled. Under these circumstances, an ongoing inflation at the expected rate develops.

To show the impact of sectoral imbalances in this case, assume, to begin with, an equilibrium inflation rate of $(\dot{P}/P)_1$. The monetary authorities are also increasing the money supply at that rate, in the absence of productivity increases or changes in velocity. In Figure 3-4, the economy is at point a on the Phillips curve denoted SS^1, at the full-employment unemployment rate, U_f. The expected inflation rate, $(\dot{P}/P)^e$, is equal to the actual inflation rate, $(\dot{P}/P)_1$. Given the level of excess aggregate demand, the occurrence of structural imbalance will raise or lower the inflation rate in the short run. Positive excess demand

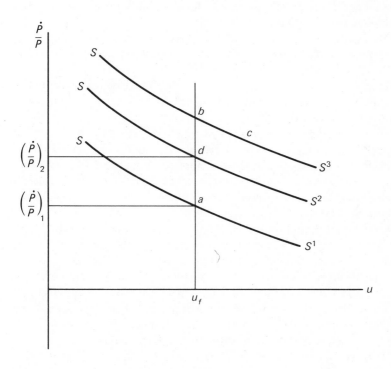

Figure 3-4. Shifts in the Phillips Curve due to Structural Inflation

in agriculture will raise the short-run inflation rate above the expected and actual $(\dot{P}/P)_1$ rate. Thus, in Figure 3-4, the Phillips curve shifts adversely from the SS^1 to the SS^3 position, for example, where the economy is now at point b with the current unemployment rate still U_f but with an inflation rate now above the $(\dot{P}/P)_1$ rate. If monetary authorities maintain the rate of monetary expansion at the original rate, increased unemployment emerges as real balances decline. That is, the economy is likely to move along the Phillips curve SS^3 to a point such as c, where both the unemployment rate and inflation rate are higher than in the original equilibrium.

In time, the spurt in the rate of change of agricultural prices is matched by a decline in the rate of change in prices elsewhere in the economy. When this occurs, the Phillips curve shifts back towards the SS^1 position. However, before the rate of price change elsewhere in the economy declines to balance the increase in the rate of price change in agriculture, the increase in the overall inflation rate may become embedded in at least somewhat higher inflationary expectations. An increase in inflationary expectations prevents an immediate shift of the Phillips curve back to the SS^1 position. If, for example, the expected inflation rate is now $(\dot{P}/P)_2$, the new Phillips curve denoted SS^2 will intersect equilibrium unemployment, U_f, at that rate.

If increased unemployment did not appear before the shift from SS^3 to SS^2, the economy would be at point d on SS^2 at the new expected inflation rate $(\dot{P}/P)_2$. But higher unemployment and lower income are likely to appear eventually, with a resulting decline in inflation. Otherwise the inflation rate and the expected inflation rate continue to be greater than the rate of monetary expansion, and real balances continue to decline.

The crucial point here is that a structurally caused change in the inflation rate will also have an impact on the level of real income. In this case, since the distribution of excess demand across sectors is such that a spurt in inflation occurs, there is a decrease in real income and an increase in unemployment in the short run. With unemployment above its equilibrium level, the inflation rate declines, bringing down the expected inflation rate as well. Eventually, inflationary expectations return to their initial $(\dot{P}/P)_1$ level. The economy is again on SS^1 at U_f. Meanwhile, however, the structural inflation has had real costs in lost output and increased unemployment. These losses can be avoided or mitigated if the government expands monetary and fiscal policy. The government can ratify any exogenous increase in the inflation rate. If it expands the rate of monetary expansion sufficiently, unemployment need not rise. Then there would be no tendency for inflation to decline either. The structurally caused spurt in inflation in this case results in a long-run increase in the inflation rate.

However, the monetarists are correct that an increase in inflation due to structural imbalances is not inevitable. There is a choice to be made. A sacrifice of output and employment for some time, the length of time depending on the strength of the structural inflation and its impact on inflationary expectations, will allow a return to the original inflation rate. If monetary policy responds passively to the higher inflation, perhaps in an attempt to avoid the short-run losses, inflation will continue at a new higher rate.

Similarly, if excess supply develops in agriculture, the argument predicts a short-run decline in the inflation rate and, if government spending is passive, a long-run decline as well. If, over time, excess supply in agriculture is balanced by excess demand, and if the government pursues a passive monetary policy, there will be no long-run impact on the inflation rate from this structuralist source. The heart of the Latin American structuralist position indicates that excess demand conditions in agriculture are more likely to occur than excess supply. If so, and if the money supply is passive, structural imbalances will result in a secular rise in the inflation rate.

III. Testable Implications of the Latin American Structuralist and Monetarist Hypotheses

The monetarist and structuralist hypotheses will be tested in Chapter 4. In this section, the testable implications of the two models are summarized. Section III.A. presents the testable hypotheses that arise out of inflation equation (1.34). The monetarist and structuralist models also have implications for the direction of causality between the money supply and prices. The testable hypotheses that this leads to are discussed in Section III.B.

III.A. Testable Implications of Structural and Demand-Pull Inflation Resulting from the Inflation Equation

In terms of the formal structuralist model derived in Chapter 1, Section III, the inflation rate varies with excess aggregate demand, here and in Chapter 4 defined, to include positive price expectations, and excess demand in agriculture in the following way:

$$\frac{\dot{P}}{P} = K_2 \frac{\Sigma P_i X_i}{\Sigma P_i \bar{q}_i} + (K_1 - K_2) \frac{P_1 X_1}{\Sigma P_i \bar{q}_i} . \tag{1.29}$$

More specifically, the structuralist model argues that, for a given level of aggregate excess demand, or for a given monetary and fiscal policy, the greater the excess demand in the agricultural sector, the higher the rate of inflation, whereas the greater the excess demand in the manufacturing and service sectors, the slower the rate of inflation. For this argument to be valid, K_1 must be greater than K_2 in equation (1.29). Prices must react more quickly in agriculture than elsewhere, and this implies that agriculture prices vary more than other prices. It is useful to examine direct evidence on the relative variation of food and nonfood prices. This is done for the Chilean economy in Chapter 4.

The reformulated Latin American structuralist hypothesis implies that the coefficient of the excess agricultural demand variable (X_1) in (1.29) is positive, because it is assumed that prices adjust more rapidly in agriculture than in other sectors. Thus, the structuralist model would be consistent with a finding of significant and positive coefficients of both terms in equation (1.29), although a strict structuralist position might imply a zero coefficient on aggregate demand variables. It is also possible to isolate a sector in which prices are commonly assumed to react more slowly than elsewhere. The structuralist hypothesis would then be consistent with a finding of a negative and significant coefficient for excess demand for this sector. The Latin American monetarist position grants a role only to excess aggregate demand in the inflationary process. The finding of a positive and significant coefficient for only the first term of equation (1.29) supports this model.

Once measures of the two terms of (1.29) are given, regression analysis can be used to test the monetarist and structuralist hypotheses. Two models of monetarist inflation have been described. These result in two possible measures of excess aggregate demand relative to output. In Chapter 1, Section III, it is indicated that the rate of change of the relative price of food, ψ, varies with excess agricultural demand, X_1, and, therefore, that ψ can serve as a proxy for X_1. The inflation rate was shown to vary with a measure of excess aggregate demand and, with ψ, as follows:

$$\frac{\dot{P}_L}{P_L} = [K_2 + fP_1(K_1 - K_2)]\frac{\Sigma P_i X_i}{\Sigma P_i \bar{q}_i} + (K_1 - K_2)\frac{P_1 e}{\Sigma P_i \bar{q}_i}\psi. \qquad (1.38)$$

For example, using Harberger's model to indicate the presence of excess aggregate demand, and assuming that full-employment income, Y_f, and inflationary expectations are unchanging, the inflation rate will equal the rate of money expansion if ψ equals zero. In a period with a shift in the concentration of excess demand to agriculture and a resulting positive ψ, the inflation rate will rise above the rate of growth of money supply. In subsequent periods, assuming ψ returns to zero, eventually, the inflation rate will again equal the rate of monetary expansion. If this rate of monetary expansion continues unchanged, the inflation rate will fall below this rate temporarily to restore the level of real balances and then continue at the constant rate of growth of the money supply.

On the other hand, if the rate of monetary expansion increases in response to the spurt in the inflation rate, a higher inflation rate will be maintained even though ψ is no longer greater than zero. Because the rise in the rate of growth of the money supply does not occur in the same period as the rise in the inflation rate, there is still room for ψ to contribute to the predictive power of the inflation equation. (In a period when the higher ψ pushes up the inflation rate, the rate of growth of the money supply is constant and so could not explain the higher inflation rate.) Only in this latter case, when government monetary and fiscal policy responds passively to prices, can structural imbalances affect the long-run inflation rate. This is discussed further in Section III.B. Moreover, the argument is symmetric. As a shift in excess aggregate demand toward agriculture raises the short-run inflation rate and, in the presence of a passive money supply, the long-run inflation rate as well, a shift away from agriculture lowers the inflation rate in the short run and possibly also the long run. The rate of change in the relative price of food, ψ, may be negative or positive. Only if ψ is predominantly positive, indicating an exogenous shift of excess aggregate demand toward agriculture over a given historical period, would its impact raise the inflation rate in that period. A passive money supply and a rise in the relative price of food are also required for support of the structuralist conclusion; thus, the presence of a positive and significant coefficient for ψ is a necessary result if the structuralist hypothesis is not to be rejected, but it is not a sufficient result.

To summarize, with the two models of demand-pull inflation, there are two ways of measuring excess aggregate demand pressures. Equation (1.29) is estimated in Chapter 4 incorporating each of these measures and using ψ to measure excess demand in agriculture. Four possible outcomes can be described. First, neither term of equation (1.29) may be significant. This outcome would support neither the structuralist nor the monetarist model. Second, the coefficients of the excess aggregate demand variables only may be significant. This would support a monetarist interpretation of Latin American inflation. Third, both terms of the inflation equation may be significant with positive signs. Fourth, the coefficient of ψ alone may be significant with the predicted sign. The fourth result would support a strict structuralist position which denies any importance to demand-pull factors while the third result would lend support to the more general structuralist model which allows the level as well as the pattern of excess demand to affect the inflation rate. However, while either of these latter two results is necessary if the structuralist argument is not to be rejected, they are not sufficient, as is discussed in the following section.

III.B. The Impact of Passive Money

An important assumption of the monetarist approach is that the money supply is exogenous. The government is viewed as setting the money supply, largely through its deficit financing of government expenditure, and thus determining the level of aggregate demand. At a given expected inflation rate, the level of aggregate demand is reflected in the unemployment rate. A Phillips-curve type of equation can then be used to determine the rate of inflation. According to the quantity theory, an exogenous money supply variable can be entered directly into the inflation equation.

In the structuralist framework, on the other hand, a passive money supply is a necessary condition for the long-run inflation rate to be affected by excess demand in agriculture. The precise mechanism through which the money supply responds to the price level, however, is not defined in the structuralist literature. In Chapter 1 it is suggested that a probable mechanism concerns the government's management of its fiscal affairs. Specifically, since the government must print money to support its fiscal expenditures, any attempt to maintain the real level of its expenditures (or deficit) in the face of a rise in the price level causes an increase in the money supply. Therefore, a rise in the relative price of food, with other prices exhibiting downward rigidity, causes an increase in the absolute price level, thus encouraging the government to increase the money supply in order to maintain its real share of national aggregate demand.

The Sims test[16] is performed to check for the existence of a passive money supply or, in other words, to analyze the feedback from the price level to the money supply. There are four possible outcomes: First, the test may indicate that an impact of money supply on prices only. Second, the test may suggest potential causality in the reverse direction only. Third, the results could indicate neither feedback from the money supply to the price level nor from the price level to the money supply. Fourth, the test may not permit us to rule out feedback in either direction.

In interpreting these results, it is necessary to emphasize that these tests do not provide direct evidence on the structure of money supply determination or of price determination. For example, a finding that money is not passively related to prices merely implies that the determinants of money supply show no consistent pattern of influence by prices. Money supply changes may be dependent on price movements. However, money supply may depend on other factors as well; for example, movements in real output, and these may swamp the influence of price movements. This also holds for the finding that prices are not influenced by money supply. Again, the impact of money supply on prices may not be seen in these results, because other factors such as fiscal policy and structural and cost-push influences are also at work. As Sims explains in his original article, "The situation is analogous to that in a supply and demand estimation problem, where we have evidence that in a particular sample elements other than price dominated supply. Such evidence proves that the price-quantity relation traces the demand curve, but it does not prove anything about the supply curve."[17]

The statistical test performed by Sims analyzed the causal feedback between nominal GNP and the money supply for the United States in the postwar period. His results permitted him to reject the notion that there had been consistent feedback from the price level to nominal output. This corresponds to the first outcome above, and supports the neoclassical assertion that the money supply can be used as an exogenous variable in an inflation equation.

If the first outcome also receives support from the Latin American data, then the quantity theory of inflation would be sustained. With an exogenously fixed money supply, changes in the relative price of food could lead to a short-run but not a long-run increase in the inflation rate. The finding of significant relative food price and excess aggregate demand variables in the inflation equation, along with the first outcome, is consistent with monetarist factors alone influencing the *long-run* inflation rate. Support for a *strict* monetarist model could be summarized as the finding of "no feedback from the price level to the money supply" *and* an insignificant relative price of food variable in the inflation equation (1.38). That is, in the short run, as well as in the long run, the rate of inflation is determined solely by demand variables. This finding of an active money supply does not necessarily mean that the monetary authorities have excessively expanded the money supply and thus created inflationary pressures. The government may have been successfully cutting back on inflation through a restrictive monetary policy. This too is consistent with the finding of an active money supply. Whatever the changes in the inflation rate positive or negative, this outcome implies that they generally arise out of changes in monetary policy. A finding of an active money supply implies that the use of money supply terms as independent variables in quantity theory inflation equations does not give rise to simultaneous equations bias.

The second outcome may be viewed as supporting a structuralist position. This finding reflects the existence of a mechanism determining the inflation rate that depends to a large extent on factors other than variations in the money supply. Such a mechanism may include significant roles for fiscal policy and for exogenous changes in price expectations, as well as for other nonmonetarist factors. Along with this result, if the relative price of food variable is a significant variable in the price equation, one could conclude that structural imbalances have a significant impact on inflation in the short run and in the long run. This second result does not imply that money supply is not important in the inflation process. Rather inflationary pressures may be provoked by nonmonetarist factors and then validated by monetary authorities. Without the validation the price level would still change in the short run, but not in the long run. Furthermore, it should be noted that a passive money supply, by itself, does not imply that inflation will increase over time. Shocks to the inflation rate arising out of exogenous shifts in the concentration of excess aggregate demand can be both negative and positive. A passive money supply policy will result in a lower inflation rate if the shocks are predominantly negative.

The third possible outcome rules out pure feedback in either direction. As does the second outcome, this implies that the rate of growth of the money supply is not an overriding influence on the inflation rate and also, as in the first outcome, that the rate of growth of the money supply is not substantially determined by the inflation rate.

The final possible outcome in testing for causality between prices and the money supply is that the evidence permits a rejection of the two distinct hypotheses of no feedback between prices and money or the reverse. First, this finding is consistent with an inflation that arises from structuralist as well as other nonmonetarist sources. A passive money supply may also occur, for example, if monetary authorities validate cost-push inflation or shifts in the expected rate of inflation due to political developments. Second, this outcome, if accompanied by the finding of significant excess demand and relative food price variables in the inflation equation, supports the hypothesis that structuralist as well as aggregate demand elements have influenced the inflation rate. This outcome and the second outcome suggest that some of the explanatory power of money supply terms in quantity theory inflation equations results from the response of money supply to exogenous price changes.

4

The Testing of Latin American Structuralist and Monetarist Theories

Introduction

In this chapter we test the monetarist and structuralist theories developed in Chapters 1 and 3. The emphasis is on testing the relevance of these hypotheses for the Chilean economy: the most well-known econometric study supporting the monetarist model was done for Chile;[1] at the same time, paradoxically, there is some agreement among structuralists that, in Latin America, the structuralist model best fits the case of Chile.[2] Section I describes and presents the results of tests employing Chilean data. However, for comparative purposes and to show the generality of the hypotheses, tests will also employ data from Argentina, Brazil, and Mexico in Section II. Section III summarizes the principal empirical findings of the chapter and presents policy conclusions. An appendix to this chapter describes and gives the sources of the data used for each country.

I. Tests of Structuralist and Monetarist Hypotheses Using Chilean Data

Introduction

In the Latin American monetarist model the inflationary process is ascribed to demand-pull factors. The Latin American structuralist hypothesis stresses the role of the relatively backward agricultural sector in inflation. In the reformulated structuralist model of Chapter 1, it is suggested that inflation may be related both to the level and distribution of excess aggregate demand, with inflation increasing, *ceteris paribus*, with the concentration of excess demand in agriculture.[a] Or, according to the price change equation derived from the reformulated structuralist theory:

$$\frac{\dot{P}}{P} = K_2 \frac{\Sigma P_i X_i}{\Sigma P_i \bar{q}_i} + (K_1 - K_2) \frac{P_1 X_1}{\Sigma P_i \bar{q}_i} . \tag{1.29}$$

---

[a]Throughout Chapter 4, the term excess aggregate demand will be defined to include inflationary expectations.

For the structuralist hypothesis of a direct relationship between excess demand in agriculture and inflation, K_1 must be greater than K_2 in equation (1.29). That is, prices must react more rapidly to excess demand in the agricultural sector of the economy than elsewhere. This assumption, while difficult to test, is examined in Section I.A. Then, in Sections I.B. and I.C., regression analysis is used to test for the significance of monetarist and structuralist factors in the inflation process in Chile. It was shown in Chapter 1 that ψ, the rate of change of the relative price of food, will vary positively with X_1, excess aggregate demand in agriculture. Then the following equation was derived to use regression analysis to test equation (1.29):

$$\frac{\dot{P}}{P} = [K_2 + fP_1(K_1 - K_2)]\frac{\Sigma P_i X_i}{\Sigma P_i \bar{q}_i} + \frac{(K_1 - K_2)P_1 e}{\Sigma P_i \bar{q}_i}\ \psi, \qquad (1.38)$$

which implies, if the reformulated structuralist hypothesis is correct, that the coefficient of ψ, the rate of change of the relative price of food, will be positive and significant. In the Latin American monetarist model of inflation, only demand-pull variables would be important in explaining the inflation rate. Hence, the coefficient of ψ in (1.38) should be insignificantly different from zero. In Section I.B., the Harberger model is employed to measure demand-pull and expectational pressures. Section I.C. specifies a Phillips-curve type of equation and tests the monetarist and structuralist hypotheses using this approach.

The monetarist and structuralist hypotheses also have differing implications for the role of the money supply in the inflationary process. In Section I.D., these implications are discussed; and the Chilean money supply and price data are then subjected to the Sims test for the existence of passive and/or active money to determine whether either or both of the hypotheses are supported by the evidence.

I.A. The Assumption of Greater Food
Price Flexibility

An indirect test of the assumption that food prices react more rapidly to excess demand than other prices is performed by examining the variance of food prices and other prices. If prices adjust more quickly in agriculture than elsewhere, agricultural prices should vary more than other prices. For several reasons, however, this test is inconclusive. First, since the consumer price index is averaged over more commodities, it would be expected to have a lower variance, due to the law of large numbers. Hence, the variance of the consumer price index should be higher than the variance of food prices by some factor. If all prices were independent, this factor would be $1/n$, where n is agriculture's share of output; and if all prices were perfectly dependent, this factor would be one. Since in Chile, over the period 1940-1970, agriculture's share of output has averaged twenty percent, the variance of overall prices should be higher than the variance of food prices by a factor between one and five. Furthermore, since the variance of the two indices reflects the respective elasticities as well as the adjustment coefficients of food prices and overall prices, only if the elasticities were comparable would the variance reflect the size of the adjustment coefficients alone. Thus, if it is found that overall prices vary more than food prices, this does not necessarily imply that food prices do adjust more rapidly. The variance of food and nonfood prices are computed by regressing in turn the log of the consumer price index and that of the food component of the consumer price index against a constant, a linear trend term and a trend term squared. The variance of the residuals of each of these regressions are then contrasted. The regression results follow (t statistics are in brackets):

$$P = -1.1678 + 0.0496T + 0.0001T^2$$

$$[-7.84] \qquad [12.68] \qquad [3.63]$$

$$R^2 = 0.9870$$

$$(4.1)$$

$$FP = -0.728 + 0.0484T + 0.0001T^2$$

$$[-4.51] \qquad [11.43] \qquad [3.84]$$

$$R^2 = 0.9855$$

$$(4.2)$$

where P indicates the log of the consumer price index; FP the log of the food price component of the consumer price index; T, a linear trend; and T^2, the trend squared. The variance of the residuals from the price of food regression is 0.00868. The variance of the consumer price index regression residuals is 0.00570. As discussed above, the issue of whether food prices adjust more rapidly than overall prices is not settled by this test. However, since the food price residual variance is greater than the variance of the consumer price residuals, these results do not refute the assumption, necessary for the structuralist argument, that prices adjust more rapidly to excess demand in agriculture than elsewhere.

*I.B. A Test of the Monetarist and
Structuralist Hypotheses Using
the Harberger Equation*

In Harberger's model, inflation is the result of an excess supply of money.

The rate of change in the demand for money at a given price level is determined by the rate of growth of real income, and the change in the cost of holding money, where the cost of holding money is represented by the inflation rate. The rate of change in the money supply is determined by the monetary and fiscal authorities. Prices then adjust to equate the demand for money to the supply. Since Harberger assumes that prices adjust over time, he enters his money supply variables with a distributed lag. Thus he proposes the following inflation equation, to be tested with quarterly data:

$$P'_t = S'_t + \beta_1 Y'_t + \beta_2 M'_t + \beta_3 D'_t + \beta_4 A'_t$$

where P'_t equals the percentage change in price level within each quarter; Y'_t equals the percentage change in real income from the past to the current quarter; M'_t equals the percentage change in the money supply in the six months ending with the end of quarter t; D'_t equals a distributed-lag weighted average of the three past values of M'_t; A'_t equals the percentage change in the general price level in the year ending at the beginning of the current quarter minus the percentage change in the general price level in the year before that; and S'_t equals a vector of seasonal constants.

Harberger's model then predicts the following coefficients for these variables: First, the coefficient of Y'_t will be insignificantly different from minus one, implying that, *ceteris paribus*, a one percent increase in the growth of real income will lead to a one percent decline in the inflation rate. Second, the sum of the coefficients of M'_t plus D'_t will be insignificantly different from 0.5, implying that, *ceteris paribus*, a one percent increase in the quarterly rate of growth of the money supply will lead eventually to a one percent growth in the quarterly inflation rate. And, finally the coefficient of A'_t will be significant and positive. The reformulated structuralist model of Chapter 1 suggested that if prices react more rapidly in agriculture than elsewhere, the inflation rate will be affected not only by the potential excess supply of money as Harberger hypothesizes, but also by the distribution of excess aggregate demand. More specifically, the inflation rate will increase to the extent excess demand occurs in the agricultural sector. And, since the rate of change in the relative price of food was seen to vary with excess demand in agriculture, the inflation rate then will vary both with excess aggregate demand and with ψ, the rate of change in the relative price of food. Thus, according to the reformulated structuralist hypothesis, inflation is determined as follows:

$$\frac{\dot{P}}{P} = [K_2 + fP_1(K_1 - K_2)] \frac{\Sigma P_i X_i}{\Sigma P_i \bar{q}_i} + (K_1 - K_2) \frac{P_1 e}{\Sigma P_i \bar{q}_i} \psi \ . \quad (1.38)$$

Since ψ, the rate of change in the price of food relative to other prices, is defined as $d(P_1/P_2)/dt/(P_1/P_2)$, ψ will move with $d[P_1/(P_1, P_2)]/dt/[P_1/(P_1, P_2)]$, the rate of change in the price of food relative to *all* prices. In the estimation of inflation equation (1.38) this latter formulation of ψ is used. That is, the relative price of food, $P_1/(P_1 + P_2)$ = FPI/CPI, is found by dividing the food price component, FPI, of the consumer price index, CPI, by the CPI. Then, the ψ (t) variable included in the estimation of the inflation equations is the quarterly rate of change in the price of food relative to all prices; that is, ψ equals

$$\frac{\dfrac{FPI}{CPI}(t) - \dfrac{FPI}{CPI}(t\text{-}1)}{\dfrac{FPI}{CPI}(t)}$$

As Chapter 1 points out, potential excess aggregate demand is measured by Harberger's variables and, if Harberger's assumptions are correct, these variables should appear with the coefficients his model predicts and the coefficient of ψ should be insignificantly different from zero. On the other hand, if the reformulated structuralist hypothesis is correct, the coefficients of both the demand-pull variables and of ψ should be significant with the anticipated signs. Hence, to test for the existence of demand-pull and structural elements in the inflation process the Harberger equation is run without and then with the rate of change of the relative price of food, ψ. The regressions use quarterly and annual data, first for the years of Harberger's study, 1940-1958, and then for the years 1940-1970.

Results using Quarterly Data for 1940-1958. The results employing quarterly data follow for 1940-1958, using only Harberger's variables (standard errors appear in parentheses):

$$P'_t = S'_t - 0.65Y'_t + 0.24M'_t + 0.21D'_t \qquad \bar{R}^2 = 0.51$$
$$ (0.155) \quad (0.059) \quad (0.075) \qquad \text{D.W.} = 1.74$$

$$(4.3)$$

$$P'_t = S'_t - 0.31Y'_t + 0.26M'_t + 0.26D'_t + 0.15A'_t$$
$$ (0.173) \quad (0.060) \quad (0.070) \quad (0.041)$$
$$\bar{R}^2 = 0.58$$
$$\text{D.W.} = 1.83^b$$

$$(4.4)$$

---

[b] The seasonal constants are insignificant in the equations that employ data from

For comparison, the results Harberger arrives at when estimating these equations are reproduced here:

$$P'_t = S'_t - 0.63Y'_t + 0.32M'_t + 0.27D'_t$$
$$\qquad\qquad (0.22)\qquad (0.09)\qquad (0.10)$$

$$\bar{R}^2 = 0.52$$

$$(2.15)$$

$$P'_t = S'_t - 0.49Y'_t + 0.33M'_t + 0.26D'_t + 0.05A'_t$$
$$\qquad\qquad (0.24)\qquad (0.09)\qquad (0.10)\qquad (0.03)$$

$$\bar{R}^2 = 0.54$$

$$(2.16)$$

The results of equation (4.3) are similar to the results that Harberger gets from equation (2.15). However, the results of equation (4.4) do not duplicate the results of Harberger's regression of these same variables. They differ in that the A'_t variable is insignificant in (2.16). The price data used here are somewhat different than the data series employed by Harberger, which may explain this divergence. The results of (4.3) and (4.4) substantially confirm the monetarist hypothesis. The coefficients of all variables are significant and appear with the expected signs. In both equations, the sums of b_2 and b_3, the coefficients of the money supply variables do not significantly differ from 0.5. This is seen by computing the confidence interval, $b_2 + b_3 \pm 1.96\, s_{b_2\, b_3}$ where $s_{b_2\, b_3}$ is equal to the square root of the sum of the variance of each of the coefficients plus twice $m_{b_2 b_3}$, the coefficients' covariance. In (4.3), $m_{b_2\, b_3}$ equals -0.0013, and $s_{b_2\, b_3}$ equals 0.081; and in (4.4), $m_{b_2\, b_3}$ equals -0.0011, and $s_{b_2\, b_3}$ equals 0.079; so that, in both equations, the ninety-five percent confidence intervals on the sums of b_2 and b_3 include 0.5. Again, in both equations, the coefficient of the income variable is significant and negative as expected indicating that a rise in real income leads, *ceteris paribus*, to a decline in prices. However, as in Harberger's estimations, the coefficients of real income are significantly smaller than unity and so do not conform in this respect to the model's predictions.[c]

1940-1958 (4.3 through 4.6, and 4.5′) except for the negative coefficient for the first quarter of the year in the equations which include the A'_t variable, (4.4) and (4.6).

[c]Harberger attributes this to the possibility that the level of real income affects the inflation rate over time as does the rate of monetary expansion. He does not attempt to correct for this by including income in the form of a distributed lag because the quarterly real income data is a constructed series, arrived at, in the first place, by interpolating the annual data.

Harberger's equations are then augmented to include the rate of change of the relative price of food, with the following results:

$$P'_t = S'_t - 0.64Y'_t + 0.25M'_t + 0.24D'_t + 0.41\psi_t$$
$$(0.145) \quad (0.062) \quad (0.069) \quad (0.118)$$

$$\bar{R}^2 = 0.58$$
$$\text{D.W.} = 1.69$$
$$m_{b_2 b_3} = -0.001135$$

$$(4.5)$$

$$P'_t = S'_t - 0.33Y'_t + 0.25M'_t + 0.29D'_t + 0.36\psi_t + 0.13A'_t$$
$$(0.160) \quad (0.058) \quad (0.067) \quad (0.110) \quad (0.038)$$

$$\bar{R}^2 = 0.64$$
$$\text{D.W.} = 1.77$$
$$m_{b_2 b_3} = -0.000978$$

$$(4.6)$$

The Durbin-Watson statistic of equation (4.5) is in the indeterminate range, indicating the possibility of first-order positive correlation of the residuals and standard errors that are biased downward. Therefore, it is appropriate to re-estimate the equation using the Cochrane-Orcutt procedure. The results follow (ρ indicates the autocorrelation coefficient and $\bar{R}^2_u$, the variance of the equation explained by the independent variables, not including the autocorrelation coefficient):

$$P'_t = S'_t - 0.62Y'_t + 0.24M'_t + 0.23D'_t + 0.42\psi$$
$$(0.161) \quad (0.066) \quad (0.078) \quad (0.116)$$

$$\bar{R}^2 = 0.58 \qquad \bar{R}^2_u = 0.57$$
$$\text{D.W.} = 1.73 \quad \rho = 0.155$$
$$m_{b_2 b_3} = -0.000795$$

$$(4.5')$$

The coefficients of the variables of equations (4.3) and (4.4) remain substantially unchanged in equations (4.5') and (4.6) when the structuralist variable ψ is

included.[d] However, this variable is also significant and positive as predicted in
the structuralist model. These results support the reformulated structuralist
hypothesis that the extent of excess aggregate demand and its concentration in
agriculture affect the inflation rate.[e]

Results Using Quarterly Data for the Period 1940-1970. Similar results
were obtained when data for 1940-1970 were used:

$$P'_t = S'_t - 0.92Y'_t + 0.26M'_t + 0.12D'_t$$

$$\qquad\qquad\quad (0.240) \quad\ (0.058) \quad\ (0.066) \quad \bar{R}^2 = 0.30$$

$$\text{D.W.} = 1.42$$

$$m_{b_2 b_3} = -0.00815$$

$$(4.7)$$

----

[d]In equations (4.5') and (4.6), the coefficients of the money supply variables are still
significant and positive and their sum is again insignificantly different from 0.5; the coefficient of income and the cost-of-holding-money variables enter significantly with the
expected signs as in (4.3) and (4.4) and the income variable again differs significantly from
minus one.

[e]There is a difficulty in interpreting the size of the coefficient of ψ, the rate of change
in the relative price of food. Since ψ is itself a function of excess aggregate demand (as is
X_1), it is not exogenous. In fact, if agriculture prices adjust more rapidly than other prices,
agriculture will be a leading sector. That is, in an excess aggregate demand-caused spurt in
inflation, food prices will go up first. The relative price of food will then rise; and, there will
be a positive correlation between the rate of change in relative food prices and the inflation
rate. However, if excess aggregate demand continues at the same level, the inflation rate will
persist at the new level, but, the relative price of food will drop to its original level. In the
following periods, the higher level of inflation will be correlated with a negative rate of
change in the relative price of food. Thus, on balance, no positive correlation results between
ψ and the inflation rate because agriculture is a leading sector, unless an increase in aggregate demand and the inflation rate is followed by a decrease in aggregate demand and
the inflation rate, *before* relative food prices can adjust back to their original level. Under
this circumstance of a gyrating excess aggregate demand and inflation rate, when agriculture
is a leading sector, the size of the coefficient of ψ will be biased upward. The size of the
independent influence of the distribution of excess aggregate demand on inflation will then
be overstated by the coefficient of ψ in the inflation equation. But agriculture can be a
leading sector only if prices adjust more rapidly in agriculture than elsewhere. Thus, the
attribution of a positive coefficient of ψ to the influence of excess aggregate demand on
both the inflation rate and the rate of change in the relative price of food is based on the
assumption that prices in agriculture are more flexible than other prices. If this assumption
is correct, the distribution of excess aggregate demand will have an impact on the inflation
rate, as the structuralists claim, although the impact will be overstated by the coefficient of
ψ, in the case of fluctuating aggregate demand.

$$P'_t = S'_t - 0.39Y'_t + 0.25M'_t + 0.16D'_t + 0.18A'_t$$
$$ (0.228) \quad (0.051) \quad (0.059) \quad (0.031)$$

$$\bar{R}^2 = 0.47$$
$$D.W. = 1.66$$
$$m_{b_2 b_3} = -0.000580$$

$$(4.8)$$

$$P'_t = S'_t - 0.90Y'_t + 0.24M'_t + 0.16D'_t + 0.14\psi_t$$
$$ (0.217) \quad (0.053) \quad (0.064) \quad (0.065)$$

$$\bar{R}^2 = 0.40$$
$$D.W. = 1.40$$
$$m_{b_2 b_3} = -0.000734$$

$$(4.9)$$

$$P'_t = S'_t - 0.45Y'_t + 0.23M'_t + 0.18D'_t + 0.13\psi_t + 0.16A'_t$$
$$ (0.217) \quad (0.076) \quad (0.054) \quad (0.062) \quad (0.029)$$

$$\bar{R}^2 = 0.53$$
$$D.W. = 1.58$$
$$m_{b_2 b_3} = -0.000631^{\text{f}}$$

$$(4.10)$$

These results broadly parallel those arrived at for 1940-1958. The monetarist variables — current and lagged money supply, real income, and the change in the inflation rate — are significant with the expected signs in each equation. The sums of the coefficients of M'_t and D'_t in each equation are not significantly different from 0.5. Again, the coefficient of the structuralist variable, ψ, the rate of change in the relative price of food, is also significant with the anticipated positive sign. These results for 1940-1970 differ from those in the shorter period only in that the absolute size of the coefficient of real income is larger if the A'_t variable is not included, so that in equations (4.7) and (4.9), these coefficients are insignificantly different from minus one. However, the Durbin-Watson statistics

---

[f]The seasonal constants are insignificant in these equations estimated over 1940-1970 except for a positive coefficient for the second quarter of the year in equations (4.7) and (4.7') which include only the money supply variables and real income.

for each of these equations are in the indeterminate range. This suggests that here also positive first-order linear correlation of the residuals may exist. The equations can be reestimated again making use of the Cochrane-Orcutt procedure to adjust for this possible problem. The results follow:

$$P'_t = S'_t - 0.7904Y'_t + 0.2180M'_t + 0.1078D'_t$$
$$\quad\quad\quad (0.2762)\quad\quad (0.0635)\quad\quad (0.0831)$$

$$\bar{R}^2 = 0.36 \quad \bar{R}^2_u = 0.30$$
$$\text{D.W.} = 2.01 \quad \rho = 0.30$$
$$m_{b_2 b_3} = 0.000004$$

$$(4.7')$$

$$P'_t = S'_t - 0.3625Y'_t + 0.2342M'_t + 0.1549D'_t + 0.1864A'_t$$
$$\quad\quad\quad (0.2480)\quad\quad (0.05365)\quad\quad (0.0666)\quad\quad (0.0347)$$

$$\bar{R}^2 = 0.48 \quad \bar{R}^2_u = 0.47$$
$$\text{D.W.} = 1.93 \quad \rho = 0.17$$
$$m_{b_2 b_3} = -0.000413$$

$$(4.8')$$

$$P'_t = S'_t - 0.6914Y'_t + 0.2076M'_t + 0.1380D'_t + 0.1345\psi_t$$
$$\quad\quad\quad (0.2597)\quad\quad (0.0596)\quad\quad (0.0797)\quad\quad (0.0650)$$

$$\bar{R}^2 = 0.46 \quad \bar{R}^2_u = 0.39$$
$$\text{D.W.} = 2.06 \quad \rho = 0.34$$
$$m_{b_2 b_3} = 0.000168$$

$$(4.9')$$

$$P'_t = S'_t - 0.3758Y'_t + 0.2222M'_t + 0.1737D'_t + 0.1316\psi_t$$
$$\quad\quad\quad (0.2375)\quad\quad (0.0514)\quad\quad (0.0651)\quad\quad (0.0624)$$

$$\quad\quad + 0.1679A'_t$$
$$\quad\quad\quad (0.03402)$$

$$\bar{R}^2 = 0.55 \quad \bar{R}^2_u = 0.53$$
$$\text{D.W.} = 1.95 \quad \rho = 0.21$$
$$m_{b_2 b_3} = -0.000275$$

$$(4.10')$$

These results differ from those above in two respects: First, the coefficient of the real income variable becomes insignificant in the equations (4.8$'$) and (4.10$'$) where the A'_t variable is included. Second, in equation (4.7$'$), the lagged money supply variable is no longer significant. At least one money supply variable remains significant in each equation and the sum of the money supply variables' coefficients in each equation is insignificantly different from 0.5. The coefficient of ψ also remains significant with the positive sign predicted by the structuralist hypothesis.

Diz has suggested that negative coefficients on money supply terms in an inflation equation could occur if there is "overshooting" in the response of the inflation rate to the rate of change in the money supply.[3] If so, it would be inappropriate to assume fixed positive weights on money supply variables as is done in the construction of the D'_t variable in the Harberger equation. To allow for the possibility of overshooting and to gather information on the importance of additional lags on money supply, quarterly inflation equations are reestimated for Chile for 1940-1970 using a twelve period (where each period is a quarter) Almon lag on the money supply.[4] The results follow in Table 4-1. These results largely confirm the previous findings. The ψ_t variable is positive and significant as the structuralist model predicts and the monetarist model also receives support. Also the real income variable appears with the predicted sign, although again it is not significant at the five percent level in the equations estimated with a Cochrane-Orcutt technique. The coefficients on money supply terms indicate that a substantial portion of the influence of a change in the rate of growth of the money supply occurs within the year of the change.

Coefficients of A'_t are significant and positive, again, in all cases, indicating that the change in the inflation rate over the past year may affect expectations of the future changes in the inflation rate and therefore the expected cost of holding money. This finding is consistent with the monetarist hypothesis. However, caution must be exercised in interpreting the significance of the coefficient of A'_t in this way. This term's significance may also reflect the importance of additional lags on independent variables as well as the omission of variables that are important in the inflationary process.

In summary, these regression results for Harberger's period as well as for the longer period, 1940-1970, imply that the null hypothesis, that excess aggregate demand variables as here constructed do not affect the inflation rate, can be rejected. The rate of change of the relative price of food also enters significantly with the expected sign in each of the above equations so that the null hypothesis, that the structuralist variable does not influence the inflation rate, can also be rejected. Hence, these results support the reformulated structuralist hypotheses of Chapter 1, which include the level and the extent to which excess aggregate demand is concentrated in agriculture, as determinants of the inflation rate.

Table 4-1
Chile: Inflation Equations Estimated for Chile with Almon Lags on Money Supply

1. $P'_t = S'_t + \underset{[5.77]}{0.09} A'_t - \underset{[-2.02]}{0.43} Y'_t + \underset{[3.87]}{0.23} M'_t + \underset{[4.01]}{0.13} M'_{t-1} + \underset{[2.07]}{0.06} M'_{t-2} + \underset{[0.91]}{0.03} M'_{t-3} + \underset{[0.62]}{0.02} M'_{t-4}$

   $+ \underset{[0.91]}{0.02} M'_{t-5} + \underset{[1.43]}{0.04} M'_{t-6} + \underset{[1.76]}{0.05} M'_{t-7} + \underset{[1.98]}{0.07} M'_{t-8} + \underset{[2.16]}{0.07} M'_{t-9} + \underset{[1.57]}{0.05} M'_{t-10} + \underset{[0.10]}{0.01} M'_{t-11}$

   PDL $\bar{R}^2 = 0.48$ D.W. = 1.73

2. $P'_t = S'_t + \underset{[5.52]}{0.19} A'_t - \underset{[-1.58]}{0.36} Y'_t + \underset{[3.60]}{0.22} M'_t + \underset{[3.65]}{0.13} M'_{t-1} + \underset{[1.95]}{0.07} M'_{t-2} + \underset{[0.92]}{0.03} M'_{t-3} + \underset{[0.64]}{0.02} M'_{t-4}$

   $+ \underset{[0.84]}{0.02} M'_{t-5} + \underset{[1.25]}{0.03} M'_{t-6} + \underset{[1.50]}{0.05} M'_{t-7} + \underset{[1.65]}{0.06} M'_{t-8} + \underset{[1.78]}{0.06} M'_{t-9} + \underset{[1.33]}{0.04} M'_{t-10} + \underset{[0.11]}{0.01} M'_{t-11}$

   PDL
   CORC $\bar{R}^2 = 0.48$ D.W. = 1.89

3. $P'_t = S'_t + \underset{[5.66]}{0.18} A'_t - \underset{[-2.19]}{0.46} Y'_t + \underset{[2.19]}{0.14} \psi_t + \underset{[4.15]}{0.24} M'_t + \underset{[4.29]}{0.13} M'_{t-1} + \underset{[2.24]}{0.07} M'_{t-2} + \underset{[1.04]}{0.03} M'_{t-3} + \underset{[0.81]}{0.02} M'_{t-4}$

   $+ \underset{[1.21]}{0.03} M'_{t-5} + \underset{[1.80]}{0.05} M'_{t-6} + \underset{[2.11]}{0.06} M'_{t-7} + \underset{[2.26]}{0.07} M'_{t-8} + \underset{[2.32]}{0.07} M'_{t-9} + \underset{[1.42]}{0.04} M'_{t-10} - \underset{[-0.24]}{0.01} M'_{t-11}$

   PDL
   CORC $\bar{R}^2 = 0.50$ D.W. = 1.76

Table 4-1 (Cont.)

4. $P'_t = S'_t + \underset{[5.43]}{0.19}\, A'_t - \underset{[-1.72]}{0.39}\, Y'_t + \underset{[2.15]}{0.14}\, \psi_t + \underset{[3.92]}{0.24}\, M'_t + \underset{[3.98]}{0.13}\, M'_{t-1} + \underset{[2.14]}{0.07}\, M'_{t-2} + \underset{[1.06]}{0.04}\, M'_{t-3} + \underset{[0.81]}{0.03}\, M'_{t-4}$

$+ \underset{[1.11]}{0.03}\, M'_{t-5} + \underset{[1.57]}{0.04}\, M'_{t-6} + \underset{[1.80]}{0.06}\, M'_{t-7} + \underset{[1.91]}{0.07}\, M'_{t-8} + \underset{[1.93]}{0.06}\, M'_{t-9} + \underset{[1.20]}{0.04}\, M'_{t-10} - \underset{[-0.20]}{0.01}\, M'_{t-11}$

PDL
CORC

$\bar{R}^2 = 0.50$
D.W. = 1.95

Notes: PDL indicates estimation with a polynomial distributed lag and CORC, the use of the Cochrane–Orcutt procedure. Values of t statistics appear in brackets.

Results Using Annual Data. Harberger's equations are also estimated with and without ψ, employing annual data. The results for Harberger's period, 1940-1958, follow (standard errors appear in parentheses):

$$P_t = -1.57 \quad - \quad 0.75Y_t \quad + \quad 0.88M_t \quad + \quad 0.26M_{t-1}$$

$$(6.17) \qquad (0.39) \qquad (0.25) \qquad (0.25)$$

$$\bar{R}^2 = 0.65$$
$$\text{D.W.} = 1.94$$
$$m_{b_2 b_3} = -0.03$$

$$(4.11)$$

$$P_t = -8.87 \quad - \quad 0.11Y_t \quad + \quad 0.66M_t \quad + \quad 0.71M_{t-1} \quad + \quad 0.14A_t$$

$$(5.76) \qquad (0.48) \qquad (0.22) \qquad (0.27) \qquad (0.05)$$

$$\bar{R}^2 = 0.77$$
$$\text{D.W.} = 2.13$$
$$m_{b_2 b_3} = -0.04$$

$$(4.12)$$

$$P_t = -1.03 \quad - \quad 0.77Y_t \quad + \quad 0.81M_t \quad + \quad 0.30M_{t-1} \quad + \quad 0.30\psi_t$$

$$(6.44) \qquad (0.41) \qquad (0.28) \qquad (0.26) \qquad (0.38)$$

$$\bar{R}^2 = 0.64$$
$$\text{D.W.} = 1.89$$
$$m_{b_2 b_3} = -0.04$$

$$(4.13)$$

$$P_t = -8.33 + 0.07Y_t + 0.61M_t + 0.73M_{t-1} + 0.24\psi_t + 0.14A_t$$

$$(6.04) \quad (0.47) \qquad (0.24) \qquad (0.28) \qquad (0.39) \qquad (0.06)$$

$$\bar{R}^2 = 0.75$$
$$\text{D.W.} = 2.09$$
$$m_{b_2 b_3} = -0.04$$

$$(4.14)$$

Here, P_t is the percentage change of the consumer price index. M_t is the percentage change of the quantity of money during the current period; M_{t-1} is the percentage change of the quantity of money in the past period; Y_t is the percentage change of real income; and A_t is the percentage change in the consumer price index during period $(t-1)$ minus the percentage change in the price index during period $(t-2)$. In each of these equations, the coefficient of one or both of the monetary variables is significant and their sum is insignificantly different from one; the coefficient of the income variable is not significant in equations (4.12) and (4.14) when the A'_t variable is included although it is significant and insignificantly different from minus one in equations (4.11) and (4.13); and the coefficient of the cost of holding money variable, A_t, is also significant with the expected positive sign. These results differ from those of Harberger in the insignificance of the income variable in equations (4.12) and (4.14) and in the insignificance of the lagged money supply in equations (4.11) and (4.13). (For Harberger's results, see Chapter 2, page 46.) Once again the data used is somewhat different, which may explain this divergence.

These equations are also estimated for the longer period, 1940-1970, with the following results:

$$P_t = 2.08 \quad - \ 1.03Y_t \ + \ 0.83M_t \ + \ 0.12M_{t-1}$$
$$\quad\quad (4.48) \quad\quad (0.30) \quad\quad (0.18) \quad\quad (0.18)$$

$$\bar{R}^2 = 0.62$$
$$\text{D.W.} = 1.63$$
$$m_{b_2 b_3} = -0.02$$

$$(4.15)$$

$$P_t = 0.36 \quad - \ 0.69Y_t \ + \ 0.70M_t \ + \ 0.29M_{t-1} \ + \ 0.06A_t$$
$$\quad\quad (4.28) \quad\quad (0.32) \quad\quad (0.18) \quad\quad (0.19) \quad\quad (0.03)$$

$$\bar{R}^2 = 0.66$$
$$\text{D.W.} = 1.51$$
$$m_{b_2 b_3} = -0.02$$

$$(4.16)$$

$$P_t = 2.40 \quad - \ 1.05Y_t \ + \ 0.78M_t \ + \ 0.16M_{t-1} \ + \ 0.23\psi_t$$
$$\quad\quad (4.55) \quad\quad (0.30) \quad\quad (0.19) \quad\quad (0.19) \quad\quad (0.31)$$

$$\bar{R}^2 = 0.61$$
$$\text{D.W.} = 1.60$$
$$m_{b_2 b_3} = -0.02$$

$$(4.17)$$

$$P_t = 0.69 - 0.70Y_t + 0.62M_t + 0.36M_{t-1} + 0.32\psi_t + 0.06A_t$$

$$\quad\quad (4.28)\quad (0.32)\quad\quad (0.19)\quad\quad (0.20)\quad\quad\quad (0.29)\quad\quad (0.03)$$

$$\bar{R}^2 = 0.67$$
$$\text{D.W.} = 1.47$$
$$m_{b_2 b_3} = -0.02$$

$$(4.18)$$

The coefficients of M_t and of A_t are significant and the sums of the coefficients of M_t and M_{t-1} are insignificantly different from one in all equations. Also, in all equations, the coefficient of income is significant and insignificantly different from minus one. The coefficients of the structuralist variable, ψ, the rate of change of the relative price of food are insignificant here using annual data from 1940-1970 as they are when annual data from 1940-1958 are used. Equations (4.15) through (4.18) all exhibit the possibility of first-order autocorrelation. Thus, the Cochrane-Orcutt adjustment can be used to reestimate the equations. The results are:

$$P_t = 3.97 - 0.86Y_t + 0.73M_t + 0.11M_{t-1}$$

$$\quad\quad (5.37)\quad (0.26)\quad\quad (0.18)\quad\quad (0.18)$$

$$\bar{R}^2 = 0.63 \quad\quad\quad \bar{R}_u^2 = 0.60$$
$$\text{D.W.} = 1.51 \quad\quad\quad \rho = 0.27$$
$$m_{b_2 b_3} = -0.01$$

$$(4.15')$$

$$P_t = 1.97 - 0.46Y_t + 0.61M_t + 0.27M_{t-1} + 0.06A_t$$

$$\quad\quad (5.39)\quad (0.28)\quad\quad (0.17)\quad\quad (0.18)\quad\quad (0.03)$$

$$\bar{R}^2 = 0.69 \quad\quad\quad \bar{R}_u^2 = 0.65$$
$$\text{D.W.} = 1.43 \quad\quad\quad \rho = 0.34$$
$$m_{b_2 b_3} = -0.01$$

$$(4.16')$$

$$P_t = 5.02 - 0.87Y_t + 0.67M_t + 0.13M_{t-1} + 0.25\psi_t$$

$$\quad\quad (5.59)\quad (0.26)\quad\quad (0.18)\quad\quad (0.18)\quad\quad (0.27)$$

$$\bar{R}^2 = 0.63 \quad\quad\quad \bar{R}_u^2 = 0.59$$
$$\text{D.W.} = 1.47 \quad\quad\quad \rho = 0.31$$
$$m_{b_2 b_3} = 0.01$$

$$(4.17')$$

$$P_t = 3.12 - 0.46Y_t + 0.53M_t + 0.31M_{t-1} + 0.32\psi_t + 0.06A_t$$

$$\quad\ (5.54) \quad (0.27) \quad\ (0.17) \quad\quad (0.18) \quad\quad\ (0.24) \quad\quad (0.02)$$

$$\bar{R}^2 = 0.70 \qquad \bar{R}_u^2 = 0.64$$

$$\text{D.W.} = 1.39 \qquad \rho = 0.39$$

$$m_{b_2 b_3} = -0.01$$

$$(4.18')$$

In terms of the coefficients of the demand-pull variables, these results, using annual data for 1940–1970, are different from the results obtained from the equations estimated using annual data from the shorter period only in that the coefficient of M_{t-1} is insignificant in each equation. Otherwise, the findings are the same: The coefficients of A_t and of M_t are significant and the sum of the coefficients of M_t and M_{t-1} are insignificantly different from one in all equations. The coefficients of income are significant and insignificantly different from minus one in the equations without the A_t' variable, (4.15') and (4.17'), and insignificant in equations (4.16') and (4.18') where A_t' is included. Finally, the coefficient of the structuralist variable, ψ, is insignificant here as in the equations using annual data from the shorter period; and, the Durbin-Watson statistics of these equations—even with the use of Cochrane-Orcutt procedure to control for first-order linear correlation of residuals—are in the indeterminate range.

The annual equations for the shorter period, and the equations estimated using quarterly data for both the long and short periods, support Harberger's model of inflation. However, in none of the regressions employing annual data, is the coefficient of the ψ variable significant in contrast to the significant coefficient found for this variable when using quarterly data. Two comments can be made about these conflicting results: First, the sample size is smaller in the annual regressions so there are fewer available observations. Second, as the discussion of Chapter 2, Section IV, indicated, one would not expect the ψ variable to appear to be significant in the long run, assuming a passive or an active money supply, even if it is significant in the short run. That is, assuming that money supply is passive, a higher ψ will induce a higher inflation rate. The money supply will then grow with the price level. And, given inflationary expectations and real income, the rate of monetary expansion will reflect fully any changes in the inflation rate. If the money supply is not passive, the inflation rate varies with ψ only in the short run and not in the long run, due to the real balance effect. In the long run, then, the money supply expands in response to higher prices so that the impact of ψ on prices is masked or prices return to their initial level in spite of a higher ψ because the money supply is unchanged. If prices respond quickly to the real balance effect and/or if the money supply responds quickly to higher prices, these long-run results may be apparent within the year.

Harberger's annual regressions and the quarterly regressions using Almon lags, indicate that the bulk of the response of prices to changes in the money supply in Chile occurs within the year. Reichmann presents evidence suggesting that this is also the case for the response of money supply to prices.[5]

I.C. A Test of the Monetarist and Structuralist Hypotheses Using the Phillips-Curve Approach

In this section the Latin American monetarist and the reformulated structuralist hypotheses are tested using the Phillips-curve equation to represent the extent of demand-pull pressures. In the structuralist model as reformulated here, inflation is a function of the level and distribution of excess aggregate demand. The Latin American monetarist hypothesis grants a role only to demand-pull elements. The findings of significant coefficients with the anticipated signs for the Phillips-curve variables and of an insignificant coefficient for ψ would support this model.

Hence, the first purpose of this section is to specify a Phillips-curve inflation equation. It is then augmented by the rate of change in the relative price of food variable to test equation (1.28). In the usual specification of the Phillips curve and in the equation used here, the inflation rate is regressed against U^{-1}, the inverse of the unemployment rate. This is done because it is assumed that the negative relationship between the inflation rate and the unemployment rate is nonlinear.

Since the unemployment data is collected in December, March, June, and September and the CPI and food price data used are averages of the three months in each quarter of the year beginning in January, the inverse of the unemployment rate is essentially lagged one month and is designated U^{-1}_{t-1}.

Because the expected inflation rate, P_e, is not directly observable, it is necessary to replace P_e with a proxy variable that is observable. Here the simplest assumption that current expectations are equal to the most recent observed rate of inflation is employed. An alternative proxy (PCE) for the expected inflation rate is then formed as an average of the four preceding quarters' inflation rates with the arithmetically declining weights of 40%, 30%, 20%, and 10%. The estimated equations using quarterly data for the period 1958-1970 follow (P_t is the across-quarter inflation rate; t values appear in brackets):

$$P_t = -1.67 + 0.27U^{-1}_{t-1} + 0.48P_{t-1}$$
$$[-0.83] \quad [2.35] \quad [3.97]$$

$$\bar{R}^2 = 0.31$$
$$\text{D.W.} = 2.10$$

$$(4.19)$$

$$P_t = -0.81 + 0.20U_{t-1}^{-1} + 0.48P_{t-1} + 0.28\psi$$
$$[-0.42] \quad [1.87] \quad\quad [4.18] \quad\quad [2.59]$$

$$\bar{R}^2 = 0.38$$
$$\text{D.W.} = 1.93$$

$$(4.20)$$

$$P_t = -2.52 + 0.30U_{t-1}^{-1} + 0.53PCE$$
$$[-1.14] \quad [2.53] \quad\quad [3.12]$$

$$\bar{R}^2 = 0.23$$
$$\text{D.W.} = 1.68$$

$$(4.21)$$

$$P_t = -1.63 + 0.24U_{t-1}^{-1} + 0.51PCE + 0.24\psi$$
$$[-0.76] \quad [2.10] \quad\quad [3.09] \quad\quad [2.24]$$

$$\bar{R}^2 = 0.29$$
$$\text{D.W.} = 1.56$$

$$(4.22)$$

In the estimation of these equations, the proxy variables for the expected inflation rate make use of the lagged dependent variable. Further, as indicated in the discussion of Chapter 3, Section I.B., the unemployment rate may be viewed as an endogenous variable in the price equation. Thus, in the interpretation of the results which follow, note that there are econometric problems associated with including the lagged dependent variable, P_{t-1}, and the lagged endogenous variable U_{t-1}^{-1}. If autocorrelated residuals are present, these problems include biased estimates of the coefficients. In all of these equations the inverse of the unemployment rate and the expected inflation rate proxies appear with the expected signs and are significant in all equations. Thus, the null hypothesis, that demand-pull factors as represented here do not affect the inflation rate, cannot be accepted. The coefficient of the structuralist variable, ψ, is also significant with the expected sign in all of the estimated equations. Hence, these results support a broad interpretation of the inflationary process in which both structuralist and monetarist factors may have a role.[g]

---

[g]Unlike those equations using the Harberger model, these equations could support an alternative interpretation: The unemployment data is for Santiago and not for the rural areas of Chile. When unemployment in rural areas increases, and food prices decline because

I.D. Testing for the Direction of Causality
Between Money Supply and Prices in Chile

In the Latin American monetarist framework, inflation is the result of overly expansive fiscal and monetary policy which implies that money supply increases may lead to inflation. Structuralists do not necessarily deny that the supply of money grows along with the price level. However, they argue that the price level is exogenously determined by other factors such as excess demand conditions in agriculture and that the money supply responds. Sims offers a procedure to test for the direction of causality between two variables where the possibility of feedback in either direction exists. To derive this test, Sims shows that in a regression of an endogenous variable Y on past, current, and future values of an exogenous variable X, the future values of X will have zero coefficients, if and only if causality runs one way from X to Y.[6] That is, if causality goes from money supply to prices only, the coefficients of future money supply terms, taken as a group, in a regression of prices on money will be zero. Similarly, if causality runs from prices to money supply only, future values of prices should have zero coefficients in a regression of money on prices.

Thus there are two null hypotheses to be tested. The first null hypothesis, H_0^1, is that future values of prices, as a group, have coefficients insignificantly different from zero, in a regression of money on prices, past and future. The second null hypothesis, H_0^2, is that future values of money supply as a group have coefficients insignificantly different from zero in a regression of prices on money, past and future. These hypotheses are tested with an F-test on the coefficients of the future independent variables in regressions which include the past and future independent variables along with a constant term and a linear trend term. Sims's testing procedure is followed. To avoid serial correlation in the residuals, all variables were prefiltered with the filter Sims used. Thus, each variable in its log form $x(t)$ was replaced by $x(t) - 1.5x(t-1) + 0.5625x(t-2)$.[h]

Four outcomes can result from the testing of the two null hypotheses: First, it is possible that neither null hypothesis can be rejected. Second, it is possible that both null hypotheses H_0^1 and H_0^2 can be rejected. This is consistent with both monetarist and structuralist explanations of inflation. Third, a structuralist model would be supported if the first null hypothesis (that future prices are related to current money supply) can be rejected and if the second

---

of an excess supply of food, ψ falls and the inflation rate also declines. Thus, ψ may be operating as a proxy for unemployment in rural areas.

[h]It is hoped that with the use of this prefilter, the regression residuals would be very nearly white noise. Testing the cumulated periodogram of the residuals in the manner described by James Durbin in "Tests for Serial Correlation in Regression Analysis Based on the Periodogram of Least Squares Residuals," *Biometrika*, March, 1969, gives results that are in the indeterminate range for each equation. Thus, as in Sims' original results for the U.S., there may be, on these grounds, some bias in F-tests on regression coefficients.

null hypothesis (that future money supply is related to current prices) cannot be rejected. Fourth, a monetarist model would be supported if the second null hypothesis can be rejected and the first cannot be rejected.

Regressions were run for the period 1940-1970. Table 4-2 shows the results of the regressions of money on prices and prices on money, both with past and with past and future independent variables. Each regression includes leading and lagging values of either money or prices, a constant term and a linear trend term, with the coefficients and values of t statistics shown in Table 4-2.

The F-tests for the coefficients on the four future independent variables only, in the regressions including leading and lagging variables, are shown in Table 4-3. The null hypotheses H_0^1 and H_0^2 were rejected at the 0.05 level. These results conform to the second outcome above. The strict monetarist hypothesis of one-way causality from money supply to prices can be rejected, and the strict structuralist hypothesis of one-way causality from prices to money supply can both be rejected. The possibility that feedback occurs in both directions cannot be rejected. Passive money supply may exist. Therefore, the structuralist hypothesis that excess demand in agriculture has influenced the long-run inflation rate in Chile cannot be rejected. These results also support the monetarist conclusion that money influences prices and thus that control over money can have an impact on prices.

II. Tests of the Structuralist and Monetarist Hypotheses for Argentina, Brazil, and Mexico

Introduction

Over the twenty-five-year period from 1950 through 1975, Brazil and Argentina have had average annual inflation rates roughly equal to the thirty-five percent average annual inflation of Chile in the period 1940-1970. Mexico, on the other hand, has had a relatively low inflation rate for Latin America, one which has averaged approximately 5% annually over these years. The recent inflationary experience of Argentina has been analyzed in a number of econometric studies, principally, those of Diz and Diaz-Alejandro, which were reviewed in Chapter 2. These econometric analyses basically use extensions of the Harberger model with results that support this model in the significance of the monetarist variables. However, the Diaz-Alejandro study, unlike that of Diz, concludes that variables other than money have played an active role in the Argentinian inflation, with money responding passively. It is interesting to compare the results of inflation equations estimated here for Argentina with the somewhat conflicting results of these earlier studies. The inflationary experiences of Brazil and Mexico have not been as extensively subjected to econometric

Table 4-2

Regressions Between Past and Future Money Supply and Prices for the Period 1940-1970: Chile

				Coefficients				
On *Lag of:* 8	7	6	5	4	3	2	1	
P on *M*: Past Only	0.026 [0.286]	−0.022 [0.242]	−0.077 [−0.820]	0.114 [1.217]	0.171 [1.786]	0.035 [0.366]	0.093 [0.977]	0.218 [2.262]
P on *M*: with Future	0.013 [0.142]	−0.075 [−0.793]	−0.115 [−1.197]	0.110 [1.149]	0.107 [1.092]	−0.021 [−0.211]	0.199 [2.000]	0.241 [2.423]
M on *P*: Past Only	−0.025 [−0.238]	0.180 [1.664]	0.164 [1.510]	0.072 [0.646]	0.121 [1.04]	−0.138 [−1.255]	0.037 [0.342]	0.056 [0.521]
M on *P*: with Future	−0.088 [−0.827]	0.144 [1.333]	0.217 [2.011]	0.054 [0.494]	0.113 [0.986]	−0.212 [−1.857]	−0.049 [−0.424]	0.120 [1.054]

Notes: Values of *t* statistics appear in brackets.

analysis as that of Argentina. However, Brazil's relative success in lowering its inflation rate, with the implementation of an indexing plan in 1964, and Mexico's historically low inflation rate, along with its often noted strong agricultural sector, make their inflationary experiences particularly interesting to examine. For these reasons, and because of the importance of the economies of Argentina, Brazil, and Mexico in the Latin American region, monetarist and structuralist theories are subjected to hypotheses testing in this section, using data from these countries. Quarterly data for 1950-1974 (1950.1-1974.3) are employed.

In Section II.A., inflation equations are estimated using the Harberger quantity theory of money model augmented by a rate of change in a relative price variable to test for the significance of the structuralist hypothesis. The reformulated structuralist hypothesis implies that the coefficient of ψ, the rate of change of the relative price to food should be positive. If subscript 1 indicates a sector where prices move more slowly than elsewhere, the coefficient on $\psi = [(\dot{P}_1/P_1) - (\dot{P}/P)]$ should be negative according to this theory. This is also tested.

In Section II.B., the Sims procedure is used to test for the existence of passive monetary policy in these countries. Again quarterly data is used for the regression analysis which is done for the period 1950.1-1973.3. Section III summarizes these and the estimated inflation equations' results and discusses policy implications.

Table 4-2 (Cont.)

					On Trend	On Constant	R^2	D.W.
			Coefficients					
0	-1	-2	-3	-4				
0.204 [2.077]					0.001 [0.653]	- 0.203 [-12.599]	0.9327	2.2972
0.135 [2.423]	0.155 [1.360]	0.145 [1.499]	-0.120 [-1.248]	0.109 [1.226]	0.001 [0.092]	- 0.201 [-12.691]	0.9359	2.3122
0.097 [0.917]					0.002 [2.627]	0.097 [1.808]	0.9374	2.3500
0.154 [1.363]	0.260 [2.409]	-0.007 [-0.071]	-0.149 [-1.391]	0.086 [0.823]	0.001 [2.048]	0.113 [2.013]	0.9393	2.4014

II.A. Inflation Equations Estimated for Argentina, Brazil, and Mexico

The results of estimating Harberger inflation equations with fixed weights on money supply for Argentina, Brazil, and Mexico appear in Tables 4-4 through 4-6, respectively. Tables 4-4a through 4-6a give the results of estimating these equations with Almon lags on money supply. The variables are defined as indicated on pages 84 and 91 of this chapter, with two exceptions. First, the data are deseasonalized. Second, since there is evidence that the most recent inflation rate provides a better measure of inflationary expectations than the inflation rate lagged four quarters, the A'_t term is defined as the difference in the current

Table 4-3
F-Tests on Future Quarters' Coefficients

		F^*	Degrees of Freedom
1940-1970	M on P	2.60	(4, 120)
1940-1970	P on M	2.40	(4, 120)

*F-tests are for the null hypothesis that all four future independent variables have zero coefficients. All tests are significant at the 0.05 level.

inflation rate and the inflation rate lagged one quarter.[i] Because the low Durbin-Watson statistics of the ordinary least square equations all indicate the possibility of first-order autocorrelation, the equations are reestimated, using the Cochrane-Orcutt technique.

In the Harberger equations estimated with fixed weights for Argentina, the coefficients of the change in the inflation rate, A_t', are positive and significant in each equation. The coefficients of the change in real income, Y_t', are significant and negative. The coefficient of the current money supply variable is significant and positive. These results conform to the predictions of monetarist theory. However, the coefficient of the lagged money supply term is insignificant. These results essentially hold whether the rate of change in the relative price of food, ψ_t, is included in the equations or not. As the structural theory predicts, in equations 2 and 4 in Table 4-4 which include ψ_t, the coefficients of ψ_t are positive. However, the coefficient of ψ_t is significant only at the ten percent level when the Cochrane-Orcutt procedure is employed. These results are reproduced in the equations estimated with an Almon lag on money supply except that the coefficients of the current money supply term as well as money supply terms lagged two quarters are significant. Negative coefficients appear on lagged money supply variables but none are significant.

The results for the equations estimated for Brazil also show a significant and positive coefficient for the A_t' term. The monetarist theory is also supported in Brazil by the finding of a positive and significant coefficient for, at least, one money term in each equation. On the other hand, the coefficient of the real income term, Y_t', is significant and negative only in the equations estimated using ordinary least squares. In terms of the predictions of the structuralist approach, the results for Brazil are similar to those found for Argentina: The coefficient of the ψ_t variable is positive and significant in both regressions. These results are reproduced in the equations estimated with Almon lags on money. These equations indicate that the impact of the rate of growth of the money supply on the inflation rate occurs within two years. Negative coefficients appear on money supply terms but are not significant.

The coefficients of the monetarist variables in the equations estimated for Mexico duplicate those found in the results for Brazil: The coefficient of A_t' is significant and positive. The coefficients of the money variables are positive and

---

[i]See Victorio Corbo, *Inflation in Developing Countries* (Amsterdam: North-Holland, 1974) pp. 181-183. The equations for Chile are reestimated using this definition for A_t'. The results, which are available from the author, do not differ from the results using Harberger's definition of A_t', except in the size of the coefficient of A_t' which is approximately 0.5, and, thus, significantly larger than the estimated coefficient of A_t' using Harberger's definition.

Table 4-4
Inflation Equations Estimated for Argentina with Fixed Coefficients on Lagged Money Supply

---

Equation

---

1 $P'_t =$ 2.730 + 0.435 A'_t + 0.305 M'_t + 0.041 D'_t − 0.175 Y'_t
   [2.865] [5.425]   [5.345]   [0.601]   [−4.657]

OLS
$\bar{R}^2$ = 0.4833
D.W. = 0.7793

---

2 $P'_t =$ 3.140 + 0.471 A'_t + 0.155 M'_t + 0.100 D'_t − 0.492 Y'_t
   [1.690] [10.271]   [2.573]   [0.980]   [−2.084]

CORC
$\bar{R}^2$ = 0.7080
D.W. = 1.5327

---

3 $P'_t =$ 1.945 + 0.348 A'_t + 0.295 M'_t + 0.102 D'_t − 0.981 Y'_t + 0.610 ψ_t
   [2.099] [4.375]   [5.486]   [1.526]   [−4.468]   [3.538]

OLS
$\bar{R}^2$ = 0.5397
D.W. = 0.9701

---

4 $P'_t =$ 2.973 + 0.440 A'_t + 0.159 M'_t + 0.114 D'_t − 0.0537 Y'_t + 0.200 ψ_t
   [1.680] [9.065]   [2.680]   [1.147]   [−2.296]   [1.838]

CORC
$\bar{R}^2$ = 0.7150
D.W. = 1.5665

Note: Values of t statistics appear in brackets. OLS indicates the use of ordinary least squares and CORC, the use of the Cochrane-Orcutt technique.

significant. The coefficient of the income term is not significant although negative which may reflect here as in the Brazilian results the endogeneity of this variable. As in the case for Argentina and Brazil, these results are unchanged by the inclusion of the ψ_t variable and the coefficient of this variable. Again, the coefficient of ψ_t is positive and significant as the structuralist theory predicts. As for Brazil and Argentina, the reestimation of these equations for Mexico with Almon lags does not change the results. In these equations, money supply terms lagged up to six quarters (five quarters in the equations estimated with the

Table 4-4a
Argentina: Inflation Equations with Almon Lags on Money Supply

1. $P'_t = 4.67 + 0.47\ A'_t - 1.03\ Y'_t + 0.27\ M'_t + 0.20\ M'_{t-1} + 0.13\ M'_{t-2} + 0.07\ M'_{t-3} + 0.02\ M'_{t-4}$
   [3.53]   [5.86]   [-4.36]   [4.13]   [5.73]   [3.70]   [1.95]   [0.70]

   $\quad - 0.01\ M'_{t-5} - 0.04\ M'_{t-6} - 0.06\ M'_{t-7} - 0.07\ M'_{t-8} - 0.07\ M'_{t-9} - 0.06\ M'_{t-10} - 0.04\ M'_{t-11}$
   [-0.57]   [-1.31]   [-1.50]   [-1.59]   [-1.70]   [-1.21]   [-0.42]

   PDL
   $\bar{R}^2 = 0.4978$
   D.W. = 0.81

2. $P'_t = 4.34 + 0.49\ A'_t - 0.41\ Y'_t + 0.15\ M'_t + 0.14\ M'_{t-1} + 0.11\ M'_{t-2} + 0.07\ M'_{t-3} + 0.02\ M'_{t-4}$
   [1.79]   [10.59]   [-1.71]   [2.31]   [2.77]   [2.10]   [1.35]   [0.52]

   $\quad - 0.02\ M'_{t-5} - 0.06\ M'_{t-6} - 0.08\ M'_{t-7} - 0.08\ M'_{t-8} - 0.06\ M'_{t-9} + 0.01\ M'_{t-10} + 0.10\ M'_{t-11}$
   [-0.42]   [-1.13]   [-1.38]   [-1.30]   [-0.88]   [0.07]   [1.03]

   PDL
   CORC
   $\bar{R}^2 = 0.7072$
   D.W. = 1.51

3. $P'_t = 3.35 + 0.39\ A'_t - 0.93\ Y'_t + 0.53\ \psi_t + 0.27\ M'_t + 0.20\ M'_{t-1} + 0.14\ M'_{t-2} + 0.09\ M'_{t-3}$
   [2.49]   [4.80]   [-4.09]   [2.95]   [4.20]   [6.15]   [4.23]   [2.51]

   $\quad + 0.04\ M'_{t-4} + 0.01\ M'_{t-5} - 0.03\ M'_{t-6} - 0.04\ M'_{t-7} - 0.05\ M'_{t-8} - 0.04\ M'_{t-9} - 0.03\ M'_{t-10} + 0.01\ M'_{t-11}$
   [1.31]   [0.05]   [-0.84]   [-1.14]   [-1.22]   [-1.17]   [-0.59]   [0.04]

   PDL
   $\bar{R}^2 = 0.5155$
   D.W. = 0.94

Table 4-4a (Cont.)

4. $P'_t = 3.74 + 0.46 A'_t - 0.44 Y'_t + 0.21 \psi_t + 0.14 M'_t + 0.14 M'_{t-1} + 0.12 M'_{t-2} + 0.08 M'_{t-3}$
   [1.58] [9.49] [-1.87] [1.86] [2.31] [2.93] [2.31] [1.56]

   $+ 0.03 M'_{t-4} - 0.01 M'_{t-5} - 0.02 M'_{t-6} - 0.07 M'_{t-7} - 0.07 M'_{t-8} - 0.04 M'_{t-9} + 0.02 M'_{t-10} + 0.13 M'_{t-11}$
   [0.72] [-0.27] [-1.03] [-1.31] [-1.21] [-0.72] [0.34] [1.35]

PDL
CORC

$\bar{R}^2 = 0.7150$
D.W. = 1.52

Note: PDL indicates estimation with a polynomial distributed lag and CORC, the use of the Cochrane-Orcutt procedure. Values of t statistics appear in brackets.

108

Table 4-5
Inflation Equations Estimated for Brazil with Fixed Coefficient on Lagged Money Supply

Equation

1 $P'_t = 1.678 + 0.511\ A'_t + 0.163\ M'_t + 0.258\ D'_t - 1.192\ Y'_t$
$\quad\quad\ [1.820]\ \ [5.954]\quad\quad [3.288]\quad\quad [5.361]\quad [-4.305]$

OLS $\quad\quad\quad\quad\quad\quad\quad\quad\quad\quad\quad\quad\quad\quad \bar{R}^2 = 0.6505$
$\quad\quad\quad\quad\quad\quad\quad\quad\quad\quad\quad\quad\quad\quad\quad\ \text{D.W.} = 0.7037$

2 $P'_t = 1.402 + 0.490\ A'_t + 0.084\ M'_t + 0.245\ D'_t - 0.223\ Y'_t$
$\quad\quad\ [0.756]\ \ [10.417]\quad\quad [1.596]\quad\quad [3.095]\quad [-0.651]$

CORC $\quad\quad\quad\quad\quad\quad\quad\quad\quad\quad\quad\quad\quad\quad \bar{R}^2 = 0.8117$
$\quad\quad\quad\quad\quad\quad\quad\quad\quad\quad\quad\quad\quad\quad\quad\ \text{D.W.} = 1.4456$

3 $P'_t = 1.588 + 0.416\ A'_t + 0.163\ M'_t + 0.273\ D'_t - 1.281\ Y'_t + 0.318\ \psi_t$
$\quad\quad\ [1.776]\ \ [4.586]\quad [3.388]\quad [5.806]\quad [-4.738]\quad [2.653]$

OLS $\quad\quad\quad\quad\quad\quad\quad\quad\quad\quad\quad\quad\quad\quad \bar{R}^2 = 0.6719$
$\quad\quad\quad\quad\quad\quad\quad\quad\quad\quad\quad\quad\quad\quad\quad\ \text{D.W.} = 0.7296$

4 $P'_t = 1.064 + 0.430\ A'_t + 0.077\ M'_t + 0.248\ D'_t - 0.333\ Y'_t + 0.196\ \psi_t$
$\quad\quad\ [0.882]\ \ [9.275]\quad [1.499]\quad [3.207]\quad [-0.986]\quad [2.456]$

CORC $\quad\quad\quad\quad\quad\quad\quad\quad\quad\quad\quad\quad\quad\quad \bar{R}^2 = 0.8216$
$\quad\quad\quad\quad\quad\quad\quad\quad\quad\quad\quad\quad\quad\quad\quad\ \text{D.W.} = 1.4622$

Note: Values of t statistics appear in brackets. OLS indicates the use of ordinary least squares and CORC, the use of the Cochrane-Orcutt technique.

Cochrane-Orcutt procedure) are significant and positive. Negative coefficients on lagged money supply terms appear but again are insignificant.

Table 4-7 presents the results of an additional test of the structuralist hypothesis. To the extent a sector has prices that adjust more slowly than prices in other sectors, exogenous shifts in the composition of excess aggregate demand

Table 4-5a
Brazil: Inflation Equations with Almon Lags on Money Supply

1. $P'_t = 1.78 + 0.52 A'_t - 1.11 Y'_t + 0.16 M'_t + 0.14 M'_{t-1} + 0.12 M'_{t-2} + 0.10 M'_{t-3} + 0.09 M'_{t-4}$
   [1.91] [6.04] [-3.85] [2.85] [5.00] [4.37] [3.42] [3.31]

   $+ 0.08 M'_{t-5} + 0.07 M'_{t-6} + 0.06 M'_{t-7} + 0.05 M'_{t-8} + 0.03 M'_{t-9} - 0.01 M'_{t-10} - 0.04 M'_{t-11}$
   [3.45] [3.00] [2.16] [1.55] [1.00] [-0.13] [-0.75]

   PDL

   $\bar{R}^2 = 0.64$
   D.W. = 0.72

2. $P'_t = 0.10 + 0.50 A'_t + 0.01 Y'_t + 0.04 M'_t + 0.05 M'_{t-1} + 0.06 M'_{t-2} + 0.07 M'_{t-3} + 0.08 M'_{t-4}$
   [0.05] [11.00] [0.01] [0.69] [1.07] [1.25] [1.50] [1.90]

   $+ 0.09 M'_{t-5} + 0.10 M'_{t-6} + 0.10 M'_{t-7} + 0.10 M'_{t-8} + 0.08 M'_{t-9} + 0.06 M'_{t-10} + 0.03 M'_{t-11}$
   [2.35] [2.51] [2.31] [2.05] [1.84] [1.45] [0.57]

   PDL
   CORC

   $\bar{R}^2 = 0.81$
   D.W. = 1.57

3. $P'_t = 1.84 + 0.43 A'_t - 1.24 Y'_t + 0.31 \psi_t + 0.15 M'_t + 0.14 M'_{t-1} + 0.13 M'_{t-2} + 0.12 M'_{t-3}$
   [2.04] [4.78] [-4.36] [2.56] [2.72] [5.38] [4.95] [3.95]

   $+ 0.10 M'_{t-4} + 0.08 M'_{t-5} + 0.06 M'_{t-6} + 0.05 M'_{t-7} + 0.03 M'_{t-8} + 0.02 M'_{t-9} + 0.01 M'_{t-10} + 0.01 M'_{t-11}$
   [3.70] [3.53] [2.65] [1.63] [1.00] [0.62] [0.15] [-0.10]

   PDL

   $\bar{R}^2 = 0.67$
   D.W. = 0.74

Table 4-5a (Cont.)

4. $P'_t = \underset{[0.11]}{0.25} + \underset{[8.66]}{0.44} A'_t - \underset{[-0.40]}{0.14} Y'_t + \underset{[2.48]}{0.20} \psi_t + \underset{[0.61]}{0.03} M'_t + \underset{[1.26]}{0.05} M'_{t-1} + \underset{[1.58]}{0.07} M'_{t-2} + \underset{[1.86]}{0.08} M'_{t-3}$

$+ \underset{[2.27]}{0.09} M'_{t-4} + \underset{[2.68]}{0.10} M'_{t-5} + \underset{[2.70]}{0.10} M'_{t-6} + \underset{[2.33]}{0.10} M'_{t-7} + \underset{[1.95]}{0.09} M'_{t-8} + \underset{[1.65]}{0.07} M'_{t-9} + \underset{[1.22]}{0.05} M'_{t-10} + \underset{[0.44]}{0.03} M'_{t-11}$

PDL
CORC

$\bar{R}^2 = 0.83$
D.W. = 1.53

Note: PDL indicates estimation with a polynomial distributed lag and CORC, the use of the Cochrane-Orcutt procedure. Values of t statistics appear in brackets.

Table 4-6

Inflation Equations Estimated for Mexico with Fixed Coefficients on Lagged Money Supply

Equation

1 $P'_t = -2.09 + 0.498\ A'_t + 0.238\ M'_t + 0.283\ D'_t + 0.132\ Y'_t$
   $\quad\quad [-5.147]\quad [7.404]\quad\quad [6.242]\quad\quad [6.309]\quad\quad [0.727]$

OLS
$\bar{R}^2 = 0.6229$
D.W. = 0.7132

2 $P'_t = -1.669 + 0.494\ A'_t + 0.184\ M'_t + 0.282\ D'_t + 0.068\ Y'_t$
   $\quad\quad [-2.523]\quad [13.733]\quad\quad [4.285]\quad\quad [4.433]\quad\quad [0.326]$

CORC
$\bar{R}^2 = 0.7823$
D.W. = 1.5326

3 $P'_t = -2.061 + 0.518\ A'_t + 0.239\ M'_t + 0.282\ D'_t + 0.115\ Y'_t + 0.058\ \psi$
   $\quad\quad [-5.155]\quad [7.745]\quad\quad [6.350]\quad\quad [6.386]\quad\quad [0.647]\quad\quad [2.027]$

OLS
$\bar{R}^2 = 0.6349$
D.W. = 0.7167

4 $P'_t = -1.620 + 0.508\ A'_t + 0.188\ M'_t + 0.282\ D'_t + 0.032\ Y'_t + 0.038\ \psi$
   $\quad\quad [-2.486]\quad [14.255]\quad\quad [4.471]\quad\quad [4.512]\quad\quad [0.157]\quad\quad [2.283]$

CORC
$\bar{R}^2 = 0.7917$
D.W. = 1.6457

Note: Values of t statistics appear in brackets. OLS indicates the use of ordinary least squares and CORC, the use of the Cochrane-Orcutt technique.

toward the sector should have a negative impact on the inflation rate. Since prices for housing, specifically, housing for rent, often are adjusted only annually, it can be hypothesized that prices in this sector are likely to be less flexible than prices elsewhere. A rate of change in the relative price of housing term, ψ^H_t, is constructed, and inflation equations estimated, including ψ^H_t as an independent variable and using data from Argentina and Brazil, where separate housing price indices are computed. In the estimated results for both Brazil and Argentina, the coefficients of the ψ^H_t term are significant and negative, as predicted, when the ordinary least-squares regression method is used. However, when a Cochrane-Orcutt procedure is applied, the coefficient of ψ^H_t is no longer significant, in the equation estimated for Brazil, although still negative. In the equation estimated for Argentina, the coefficient of ψ^H_t remains negative and significant only at the ten percent level, however.

Table 4-6a
Mexico: Inflation Equations with Almon Lags on Money Supply

1. $P'_t = -1.67 + 0.50 A'_t + 0.07 Y'_t + 0.16 M'_t + 0.20 M'_{t-1} + 0.20 M'_{t-2} + 0.18 M'_{t-3} + 0.15 M'_{t-4}$
    $\quad\ [-2.32]\ \ [8.29]\ \ \ \ \ [0.29]\ \ \ \ [3.40]\ \ \ \ [7.79]\ \ \ \ \ \ [9.00]\ \ \ \ \ \ [7.76]\ \ \ \ \ \ [6.65]$

    $\quad + 0.10 M'_{t-5} + 0.05 M'_{t-6} + 0.01 M'_{t-7} - 0.02 M'_{t-8} - 0.03 M'_{t-9} - 0.01 M'_{t-10} + 0.04 M'_{t-11}$
    $\quad\ \ \ [5.03]\ \ \ \ \ \ [2.46]\ \ \ \ \ [0.32]\ \ \ \ \ [-0.78]\ \ \ \ [-1.06]\ \ \ \ [-0.29]\ \ \ \ \ \ [0.95]$

    PDL
    $\bar{R}^2 = 0.63$
    D.W. = 0.79

2. $P'_t = -0.92 + 0.50 A'_t + 0.06 Y'_t + 0.10 M'_t + 0.16 M'_{t-1} + 0.19 M'_{t-2} + 0.18 M'_{t-3} + 0.15 M'_{t-4}$
    $\quad\ [-0.91]\ \ [14.43]\ \ \ \ \ [0.23]\ \ \ \ [2.07]\ \ \ \ [4.80]\ \ \ \ \ \ [5.57]\ \ \ \ \ \ [5.17]\ \ \ \ \ \ [4.38]$

    $\quad + 0.10 M'_{t-5} + 0.05 M'_{t-6} - 0.01 M'_{t-7} - 0.04 M'_{t-8} - 0.06 M'_{t-9} - 0.04 M'_{t-10} + 0.01 M'_{t-11}$
    $\quad\ \ \ [3.09]\ \ \ \ \ \ [1.41]\ \ \ \ \ [-0.07]\ \ \ \ [-1.04]\ \ \ \ [-1.49]\ \ \ \ [-1.18]\ \ \ \ \ \ [0.03]$

    PDL
    CORC
    $\bar{R}^2 = 0.77$
    D.W. = 1.46

3. $P'_t = -1.68 + 0.52 A'_t + 0.06 Y'_t + 0.07 \psi_t + 0.16 M'_t + 0.19 M'_{t-1} + 0.20 M'_{t-2} + 0.18 M'_{t-3}$
    $\quad\ [-2.39]\ \ [8.63]\ \ \ \ \ [0.29]\ \ \ \ [2.15]\ \ \ \ [3.38]\ \ \ \ [7.85]\ \ \ \ \ \ [9.12]\ \ \ \ \ \ [7.91]$

    $\quad + 0.15 M'_{t-4} + 0.10 M'_{t-5} + 0.05 M'_{t-6} + 0.01 M'_{t-7} - 0.02 M'_{t-8} - 0.03 M'_{t-9} - 0.01 M'_{t-10} + 0.05 M'_{t-11}$
    $\quad\ \ \ [6.82]\ \ \ \ \ \ [5.20]\ \ \ \ \ [2.58]\ \ \ \ \ [0.40]\ \ \ \ \ [-0.73]\ \ \ \ [-1.01]\ \ \ \ [-0.23]\ \ \ \ \ \ [1.02]$

    PDL
    $\bar{R}^2 = 0.65$
    D.W. = 0.79

Table 4-6a (Cont.)

4.

$$P'_t = -1.05 + 0.51\, A'_t + 0.05\, Y'_t + 0.05\, \psi_t + 0.10\, M'_t + 0.16\, M'_{t-1} + 0.19\, M'_{t-2} + 0.18\, M'_{t-3}$$
$$ [-1.06] \quad [15.07] \quad [0.20] \quad\quad [2.44] \quad\quad [2.05] \quad\quad [4.88] \quad\quad [5.72] \quad\quad [5.36]$$

$$+\ 0.15\, M'_{t-4} + 0.10\, M'_{t-5} + 0.05\, M'_{t-6} + 0.01\, M'_{t-7} - 0.03\, M'_{t-8} - 0.05\, M'_{t-9} - 0.04\, M'_{t-10} + 0.01\, M'_{t-11}$$
$$\quad [4.59] \quad\quad [3.31] \quad\quad [1.62] \quad\quad [0.12] \quad\quad [-0.87] \quad\quad [-1.31] \quad\quad [-0.96] \quad\quad [0.25]$$

$$\bar{R}^2 = 0.79$$
$$\text{D.W.} = 1.58$$

PDL
CORC

Note: PDL indicates estimation with a polynomial distributed lag and CORC, the use of the Cochrane-Orcutt procedure. Values of t statistics appear in brackets.

Table 4-7
Inflation Equations Estimated for Argentina and Brazil with a Lagging Sector (Housing)

Equation

Argentina:

1 $P'_t =$ 2.163 + 0.460 A'_t + 0.321 M'_t + 0.041 D'_t − 0.890 Y'_t − 0.082 ψ^H
        [2.286]   [5.881]   [5.787]   [0.622]   [−3.807]   [−2.691]

OLS $\bar{R}^2$ = 0.5155
                                                                       D.W. = 0.8626

2 $P'_t =$ 2.968 + 0.487 A'_t + 0.169 M'_t + 0.093 D'_t − 0.448 Y'_t − 0.031 ψ^H
        [1.641]   [10.479]   [2.813]   [0.929]   [−1.903]   [−1.771]

CORC $\bar{R}^2$ = 0.7145
                                                                       D.W. = 1.5535

Brazil:

1 $P'_t =$ 1.759 + 0.444 A'_t + 0.131 M'_t + 0.280 D'_t − 1.197 Y'_t − 0.103 ψ^H
        [1.989]   [5.043]   [2.619]   [5.863]   [−4.450]   [−2.302]

OLS $\bar{R}^2$ = 0.6658
                                                                       D.W. = 0.8466

2 $P'_t =$ 1.451 + 0.494 A'_t + 0.084 M'_t + 0.242 D'_t − 0.215 Y'_t − 0.006 ψ^H
        [0.779]   [9.876]   [1.576]   [3.042]   [−0.626]   [−0.203]

CORC $\bar{R}^2$ = 0.8126
                                                                       D.W. = 1.4577

Note: Values of t statistics appear in brackets. OLS indicates the use of ordinary least squares and CORC, the use of the Cochrane-Orcutt technique.

In general, the results of estimating the Harberger inflation equation for Argentina, Brazil, and Mexico support the earlier findings for Chile. In all the estimated equations, the A'_t variable is significantly positive. This is consistent with a model in which inflationary expectations are an important factor in the inflationary process, although it is also consistent with the importance of omitted variables or additional lags on variables that are included. The coefficient of at least one money supply variable is significant in all equations. Thus, for these economies, as for Chile, the monetarist hypothesis is substantially supported. Finally, as in the case of Chile, the coefficient of ψ_t is significant with the expected positive sign in all equations for Brazil and Mexico. Hence, these results suggest that in Brazil and Mexico, as in Chile, there is evidence of a broad inflationary process which, in the short run, includes both structuralist and monetarist influences.

The results for Argentina do less well in terms of the structuralist hypothesis, since the coefficient of the ψ_t term in the equations estimated using the Cochrane-Orcutt procedure is significant only at the ten percent level. In all of these equations the low Durbin-Watson statistics indicate possible serial correlation of residuals due to the exclusion of additional variables which also affect the inflation process.

II.B. Tests for the Direction of Causality between Money Supply and Prices for Argentina, Brazil, and Mexico

Results of Sims tests estimated for Argentina, Brazil, and Mexico for the period 1950.1 through 1973.3 appear in Tables 4-8 through 4-10, respectively.

The associated F-tests on the four future values of money in the regressions of prices on money and of the four future values of prices in the regressions of money on prices appear in Table 4-11. As discussed above, there are two null hypotheses to be listed: The first null hypothesis, H_0^1, is that future values of prices, as a group, have coefficients insignificantly different from zero in a regression of money on prices. The rejection of this hypothesis supports the monetarist model. The second null hypothesis, H_0^2, is that future values of money, as a group, have coefficients insignificantly different from zero in a regression of prices on money. The rejection of this hypothesis is consistent with a passively determined money supply.

The results, summarized in Table 4-11, indicate that for Brazil and Mexico H_0^2 is rejected, but H_0^1 cannot be. This suggests that, over this historical period, Brazilian and Mexican monetary authorities were passively adjusting the rate of monetary expansion in response to prices. In these countries, as in Chile, there is evidence that exogenous changes in the inflation were ratified by monetary policy. The long-run implication of the structuralist model that the distribution of excess aggregate demand has a continuing impact on inflation is consistent with this result. In addition, for Brazil and Mexico, the hypothesis that the coefficients of future values of prices, taken as a group, are zero, in a regression of money on prices, cannot be rejected. This finding further supports the structuralist model. Either money has no impact on prices or factors other than money are influencing prices to a sufficient extent that money does not appear to be significantly correlated with prices in a regression analysis which includes only money and prices.

The results for Argentina are the reverse of these. The monetarist hypothesis, that influence goes from money to prices but not from prices to money, is

Table 4-8

Regressions Between Past and Future Money Supply and Prices for the Period 1950-1973: Argentina

On				*Coefficients*				
Lag of:	8	7	6	5	4	3	2	1
P on M: Past Only	-0.099 [-0.612]	-0.228 [-1.342]	0.040 [0.235]	-0.041 [-0.238]	-0.248 [-1.464]	0.140 [0.811]	0.337 [2.169]	0.224 [2.043]
P on M: with Future	-0.108 [-0.657]	-0.205 [-1.205]	0.074 [0.423]	-0.058 [-0.220]	-0.320 [-1.846]	0.145 [0.818]	0.338 [2.133]	0.150 [1.249]
M on P: Past Only	-0.030 [-0.254]	-0.049 [-0.421]	0.170 [1.458]	-0.091 [-0.732]	0.219 [1.893]	0.087 [0.759]	-0.049 [-0.425]	0.147 [1.325]
M on P: with Future	-0.089 [-0.771]	-0.047 [-0.412]	0.161 [1.412]	-0.041 [-0.359]	0.252 [2.261]	0.023 [0.208]	-0.099 [-0.880]	0.138 [1.269]

Notes: Values of t statistics appear in brackets.

Table 4-9

Regressions Between Past and Future Money Supply and Prices for the Period 1950-1973: Brazil

On				*Coefficients*				
Lag of:	8	7	6	5	4	3	2	1
P on M: Past Only	-0.199 [-1.694]	0.018 [0.146]	0.111 [0.922]	0.223 [1.929]	0.011 [0.097]	0.181 [1.662]	0.163 [1.434]	0.062 [0.546]
P on M: with Future	-0.154 [-1.307]	0.021 [0.171]	0.132 [1.072]	0.153 [1.243]	-0.065 [-0.534]	0.073 [0.630]	0.117 [0.998]	-0.012 [-0.108]
M on P: Past Only	0.189 [1.588]	0.001 [0.012]	-0.164 [-1.382]	0.134 [1.094]	-0.031 [-0.235]	0.245 [1.982]	0.209 [1.729]	0.248 [2.053]
M on P: with Future	0.188 [1.516]	0.016 [0.131]	-0.172 [-1.400]	0.121 [0.954]	-0.011 [-0.084]	0.268 [1.945]	0.189 [1.372]	0.212 [1.548]

Notes: Values of t statistics appear in brackets.

Table 4-8 (Cont.)

					Coefficients			
0	-1	-2	-3	-4	On Trend	On Constant	$\bar{R}^2$	D.W.
0.147 [1.363]					0.003 [1.737]	-0.199 [-1.111]	0.8676	2.1642
0.215 [1.870]	0.128 [1.153]	-0.063 [-0.561]	0.142 [1.350]	0.129 [1.265]	0.002 [0.902]	-0.322 [-1.695]	0.8697	2.2212
0.049 [0.440]					0.002 [1.842]	0.428 [12.579]	0.8469	2.4515
0.059 [0.540]	0.336 [3.180]	-0.023 [-0.219]	0.051 [0.490]	-0.179 [-1.709]	0.002 [1.334]	0.435 [12.094]	0.8603	2.4894

Table 4-9 (Cont.)

					Coefficients			
0	-1	-2	-3	-4	On Trend	On Constant	$\bar{R}^2$	D.W.
0.244 [2.174]					0.001 [0.578]	-0.215 [-11.760]	0.9611	1.6917
0.145 [1.258]	0.110 [0.957]	0.087 [0.735]	0.262 [2.257]	0.178 [1.554]	-0.001 [-1.119]	- 0.254 [-12.217]	0.9648	1.9487
0.001 [0.010]					0.001 [2.015]	0.235 [13.142]	0.9682	2.1553
-0.015 [-0.112]	-0.037 [-0.283]	0.002 [0.014]	0.117 [0.945]	-0.028 [-0.225]	0.001 [2.015]	0.237 [13.142]	0.9671	2.1391

Table 4-10

Regressions Between Past and Future Money Supply and Prices for the Period 1950-1973: Mexico

				Coefficients				
On Lag of:	8	7	6	5	4	3	2	1
P on *M*: Past Only*	0.109 [0.130]	−0.072 [−0.082]	−1.637 [−1.958]	−0.286 [−0.352]	−2.990 [−3.691]	2.489 [3.130]	0.381 [0.455]	−0.562 [−0.652]
P on *M*: with Future	0.149 [0.173]	−0.052 [−0.058]	−1.838 [−2.083]	−0.072 [−0.080]	−2.942 [−3.296]	2.593 [2.990]	0.110 [0.123]	−0.309 [−0.344]
M on *P*: Past Only	−0.008 [−0.524]	0.006 [0.325]	0.008 [0.445]	0.009 [0.480]	−0.006 [−0.326]	−0.004 [−0.224]	0.017 [0.893]	0.038 [2.060]
M on *P*: with Future	−0.009 [−0.704]	0.005 [0.319]	0.009 [0.569]	0.009 [0.576]	−0.003 [−0.214]	0.001 [0.023]	0.026 [1.557]	0.051 [3.061]

Notes: Values of *t* statistics appear in brackets.

consistent with these findings. Although there is evidence that shifts in the distribution of excess aggregate demand have an impact on the short-run inflation rate in Argentina, the long-run inflation rate is unaffected. This implies that exogenous shocks on prices have been allowed to have an impact on real income. This result is consistent with Diaz-Alejandro's discussion of the large amount of variation in Argentina's income, over these years. The evidence of the Sims tests does not support the conclusion of the Diaz-Alejandro study of the importance of passive money in this period.[7]

III. Principal Results and Consequences of Results for Policy

The purpose of this section is twofold. First, in Section III.A., the principal empirical results of this chapter are summarized. Second, in Section III.B., the implications of these results for possible policies to deal with inflation are discussed.

Table 4-10 (Cont.)

					Coefficients			
0	-1	-2	-3	-4	On Trend	On Constant	$\bar{R}^2$	D.W.
1.526 [1.838]					0.002 [0.343]	0.717 [0.430]	0.2802	2.8712
1.379 [1.550]	-0.278 [-0.328]	0.704 [0.828]	-0.767 [-0.862]	0.033 [0.037]	0.003 [0.338]	0.826 [0.400]	0.2665	2.8592
0.020 [1.255]					0.002 [19.313]	0.432 [15.945]	0.8172	2.6943
0.042 [2.470]	0.035 [2.070]	0.031 [1.796]	0.061 [3.730]	-0.020 [-1.459]	0.002 [18.747]	0.391 [13.111]	0.8650	2.6405

Table 4-11
F-Tests on Future Quarters' Coefficients: Argentina, Brazil, and Mexico

F-tests are for the null hypothesis that all four future independent variables have zero coefficients.

All tests are for the regression period 1950.1-1973.3.

Country	Regression Equation	F	Degrees of Freedom
Argentina	M on P	2.97*	(4, 95)
Argentina	P on M	1.32	(4, 95)
Brazil	M on P	0.28	(4, 95)
Brazil	P on M	3.13*	(4, 95)
Mexico	M on P	0.54	(4, 95)
Mexico	P on M	2.33*	(4, 95)

*Indicates significance at the 0.05 level.

III.A. Summary of Principal Results

The empirical results of this chapter support a broad model of inflation. The findings of generally significant coefficients, with the anticipated signs for demand-pull and expectational variables in the Harberger equations estimated for each economy, are consistent with the Latin American monetarist argument that excessive expansion of the money supply is responsible for inflation. However, the relevance of the reformulated structuralist model is also substantially supported by the results of this chapter. The reformulated structuralist hypothesis states that, because agricultural prices react more quickly to excess demand than prices elsewhere, exogenous shifts in excess demand in agriculture as well as the overall level of excess aggregate demand affect the inflationary process. As Chapter 1 indicates, ψ, the rate of change in the relative price of food, varies with exogenous shifts in excess demand in agriculture, given overall aggregate demand. Thus, the reformulated structuralist hypothesis is tested by estimating an inflation equation which includes ψ as well as excess aggregate demand variables. The finding of significant and positive coefficients for ψ (along with the significant coefficients with appropriate signs for the aggregate demand variables) in the Harberger quarterly equations is consistent, therefore, with the workings of a short-run reformulated structuralist model, in Argentina, Brazil, Chile, and Mexico. For the economies of Brazil, Chile, and Mexico, the Sims tests provide evidence of a passive monetary policy. Thus, in these economies, the findings of the Sims tests and the inflation equations support the possibility that structuralist factors have a long-run, as well as a short-run, positive impact on the inflation rate.

*III.B. Consequences of the Results
for Policy*

In the reformulated structuralist model, an economy is subjected to an inflationary bias, even in the absence of excess aggregate demand, when an exogenous increase in excess demand in agriculture raises relative food prices. Since the relative price of food in Chile and Brazil has increased over time, this reflects that ψ has been positive more often than negative and, therefore, that the inflation rate in Chile and Brazil has been higher than would have been the case if purely excess aggregate demand variables were at work. That is, for the structuralist argument to be supported, agriculture's prices relative to overall prices must be rising. This has occurred in Chile and Brazil. Thus, the structuralist position on the predisposition of Latin American economies to inflation is supported for these economies. In Argentina, as well, the results of the structuralist model are supported for the short run. The relative price for food in Argentina also has increased over time. Thus, the effect of shocks deriving from the agriculture sector over this period has generally been to raise the short-run inflation rate and lower real income. The Sims test gives evidence that Argentina has not typically ratified inflation derived from exogenous shocks; rather, the shocks have been allowed to have their impact on real income. Finally, in Mexico, the relative price of food has fallen over time. Thus, the generally confirmed predictions of the reformulated structuralist model for the case of Mexico implies that that country's relatively strong agriculture sector has contributed to its low inflation rate. The contribution of the structuralist model to a description of the inflationary experience of these countries cannot be rejected. The structuralist policy prescription of the need for land reform, which increases agriculture's productivity, is also validated by the evidence for this model. However, the monetarist argument, that structuralist factors need not inevitably lead to increased inflation, is supported by this chapter's findings, as well. The results are consistent with the monetarist hypothesis that monetary and fiscal policy do have an impact on prices. In fact, money supply may be passive as the structuralists suggest, but it does not have to be. However, the importance of inflationary expectations and lagged terms means that if monetary restraint is implemented, unemployment and a slowing of growth will ensue before inflation is brought completely under control. Furthermore, the results imply that the less flexible prices outside the agricultural sector are, the more agricultural difficulties will contribute to inflationary pressures. And, in spite of monetary and fiscal policies that keep excess aggregate demand in bounds, excess demand in agriculture can raise the short-run inflation rate. Thus, policies that control inflationary expectations, and that discourage monopoly power, and that improve agricultural productivity, will also have an impact, along with the traditional policies of monetary and fiscal restraint, in limiting the inflationary process.

IV. Appendix

The hypotheses tested in this chapter use data from Chile, Argentina, Brazil, and Mexico. Sources and descriptions of Chilean data are given in Section IV.A. The sources and description of data from Argentina, Brazil, and Mexico are found in Section IV.B. Tables of the data appear at the end of Section IV.B.3.

IV.A. Sources and Description of the Chilean Data

The hypotheses discussed in Chapter 3, Section IV, are tested using data from Chile on money, prices, unemployment, and income. The principal source of these data series is the *Boletin Mensual* of the Banco Central de Chile.

IV.A.1. National Income Data For Chile. The Corporacion de Fomento de la Produccion (CORFO), Direccion de Planeficacion, Departamento de Investigaciones Economicas, an agency of the Chilean government, has made estimates of Chile's real national income, on an annual basis, for 1940-1960. For the years since 1960, the estimation of annual real national income statistics has been a function of ODEPLAN, Presidencia de la Republica. Each year revisions have been made in the estimated national income of previous years. The index of output used in this study is from data given by CORFO in its latest (1961) publication for 1940-1960 and since 1960 from the updated figures provided by ODEPLAN. Both series are published in the *Cuentas Nacionales de Chile.*

In attempting to reproduce Harberger's results for his inflation equation for 1940-1958, quarterly national income data that Harberger provides are used. The complicated derivation procedure which he uses to interpolate quarterly income data from the national income series is described in an appendix to his study.[8]

Quarterly income statistics are derived from the annual data, for the longer period 1940-1970, in a method suggested by Diz:[9] Quarterly figures are found through linear interpolation of the annual data when the sum of the quarterly changes in income over the year is constrained to add up to the annual change in income. That is, the following equations are used:

$$q_1^t = \left[\frac{4y_t}{\Sigma q_i^t} \, y_{t-1} + \frac{7.5}{12} \, (y_t - y_{t-1}) \right]$$

$$q_2^t = \left[\frac{4y_t}{\Sigma q_i^t} \, y_{t-1} + \frac{10.5}{12} \, (y_t - y_{t-1}) \right]$$

$$q_3^t = \left[\frac{4y_t}{\Sigma q_i^t} \, y_t + \frac{1.5}{12} \, (y_{t+1} - y_t) \right]$$

$$q_4^t = \left[\frac{4y_t}{\Sigma q_i^t} \, y_t + \frac{4.5}{12} \, (y_{t+1} - y_t) \right]$$

where y_t denotes real income in year t and q_i^t, real income for quarter i of year t.

IV.A.2. Unemployment Data for Chile. The unemployment data is developed by the Instituto de Economia, Universidad de Chile from a household labor force survey for the Greater Santiago area. (Greater Santiago accounted for forty-five percent of the Chilean urban population and fifty percent of its labor force in 1967.)[10] Data on labor supply, employment, and population are collected in March, June, September, and December of each year, beginning with June 1960. Semiannual data were collected in 1958 and 1959. The data are reported in *Ocupacion y Desocupacion*, Gran Santiago, various issues, published in Santiago, Chile, by the Instituto de Economia. The population data are broken down between men and women, between those under and over fourteen years of age, and between those in the labor force and those who are not seeking work. The labor force is further broken down between the employed and the unemployed. The employed category is divided into those who are working and those who are temporarily absent from their jobs. The unemployed category is divided between those who are moving from one job to another and those who are looking for work for the first time. For this study, to derive unemployment statistics, labor supply are those reported in the labor force and labor demand are the employed workers. The unemployment rate is then calculated as total labor force minus the employed, divided by the total labor force. Occasionally the Instituto de Economia revises previously reported statistics. In these cases the updated figures are used.

IV.A.3. Price Data for Chile. Data on prices are derived from the consumer price index for Santiago prepared by the Banco Central de Chile since 1928. The price index is provided in monthly form. An averaging procedure is used to calculate a quarterly series. The food price component of the consumer price index of Santiago is used to derive the relative price of food. Both series are published by *Boletin Mensual* of the Banco Central. In 1959, the Banco Central revised several prior consumer price series to derive a consistent series for 1928-1958. In this recomputed series 1958 commodity weights are used.[11]

IV.A.4. Money Supply Data for Chile. The Banco Central de Chile publishes in the *Boletin Mensual* monthly statistics on the money supply. By averaging the monthly statistics a quarterly series is obtained. The series used for the money supply is that for the "total del dinero circulante." This series is provided in a consistent form from 1948 on. It includes currency outside of banks, demand deposits in commercial banks (including float and deposits of the government and excluding interbank deposits), and deposits of government and semifiscal agencies in the central bank. Prior to 1948, the money supply data is provided in a slightly different form. For 1935-1944, data are given on currency outside of banks on a monthly basis and data on demand deposits only on a semiannual basis. The latter series is interpolated in this study to provide quarterly statistics. Also prior to 1948 money supply data do not include government deposits in the central bank. In periods of overlap in the different series the latest data are used.

IV.B. Sources and Description of the Data from Argentina, Brazil, and Mexico

The equations for Argentina, Brazil, and Mexico are estimated in quarterly form using data on income, prices, and money supply. Income data for each country is available only in annual form. In each case, the annual income data is interpolated to provide quarterly data by the method suggested by Diz, described above in Section IV.A. Money supply and price data are collected for the three countries in monthly form. More detailed discussion of the form and sources for the data from each of the countries follows.

IV.B.1. Argentina. Price data for Argentina are derived from the cost-of-living index published by the National Bureau of Statistics and the Census in the *Sintesis Estadistica Mensual de la Republica Argentina.* The statistics are based on the living expenses of an unskilled industrial worker with a wife and two children living in the city of Buenos Aires. The index is computed using 1960 as a base; this is linked to an index using 1943 as a base for the earlier years. The housing (*alojamiento*) and food (*alimentacion*) components of this index are used to derive the relative prices of housing and food. The statistics are published in a monthly form and are averaged to calculate a quarterly series.

Money supply data for Argentina are taken from a series published by the Banco Central de la Republica Argentina in the *Boletin Estadistico.* An end-of-quarter series is used which includes billetas y monedas (currency outside of banks) and cuentas corrientes (demand deposits).

Annual income data for Argentina are derived from the gross national income series calculated in 1960 prices by the Banco Central de la Republica Argentina. These are published in the *Boletin Estadistico.* Quarterly income statistics are formulated from the annual data by the method discussed above. (See page 122).

IV.B.2. Brazil. Price data for Brazil are prepared by the Instituto Brasileiro de Economia (IBRE) and published by *Conjuntura Economica.* The monthly cost-of-living index for Guanabara, with a base period of 1965-1967, is averaged to provide a quarterly price index.

The foodstuffs (*alimentacao*) and housing (*habitacao*) components of the cost-of-living index are used to construct the relative price of food and housing series.

Monthly money supply series for Brazil are supplied by the Banco Central do Brasil. The series used, *meios de pagamiento,* include currency held by the public and checking accounts in commercial banks and the Banco de Brasil. The series used is a revised one published in monthly form in the January 1975 *Conjuntura Economica* and is averaged to provide quarterly data.

Estimates of gross domestic product in Brazil are gathered by the Centro de Contas Nacionals and are published in *Conjuntura Economica*. This annual series is interpolated to arrive at a quarterly series in the manner described above.

IV.B.3. Mexico. Money supply data and price data for Mexico are gathered by the Banco de Mexico in monthly form. These are averaged to provide quarterly statistics. The money supply series used is *"medio circulante"* which includes checking accounts and currency in the hands of the public. The overall price index used is the *indice de precios al mayoreo en la ciudad de Mexico* (wholesale price index for Mexico City). The base of the index is 1954. The food price index used to construct the relative price of food is taken from the food price component (*alimentos*) of the wholesale price index. These data on money supply and prices are published in the *Asamblea General Ordinaria de Accionistas* before 1972 and, from 1972 on, are in *Indicadores Economicos*.

Income data for Mexico are derived from an annual series compiled by the Wharton Econometric Forecasting Associates. The series used is that of the gross domestic product in 1950 prices. The data are interpolated (see page 122) to provide quarterly data.

Table 4-12
Indexes for Argentina for 1947–1974

Period	General Price Index	Money Supply	Housing Price Index	Food Price Index	Change In Real Income
1947.3	4.700	9198.000			
1947.4	4.800	10247.000			
1948.1	4.900	10856.000			
1948.2	5.100	11542.890			
1948.3	5.300	12232.300			
1948.4	5.700	13771.390			
1949.1	6.000	14883.100			
1949.2	6.700	14996.190		46.880	
1949.3	7.100	15404.690	5.100	46.880	
1949.4	7.600	17577.500	5.800	46.960	
1950.1	7.800	17984.600	6.100	46.950	
1950.2	8.400	18888.890	6.700	50.930	0.595
1950.3	8.800	19629.890	7.500	50.930	-0.069
1950.4	9.400	22048.690	7.900	50.950	0.413
1951.1	9.600	23386.000	8.000	50.930	0.887
1951.2	11.300	23818.300	8.400	50.930	2.772
1951.3	12.600	24631.100	9.500	50.930	0.872
1951.4	13.600	26744.600	11.100	50.970	-0.573
1952.1	15.100	26500.690	12.300	51.010	-2.065
1952.2	16.700	26687.100	13.600	51.170	-5.831
1952.3	16.500	27214.100	15.400	51.170	-2.154
1952.4	17.000	30415.690	15.200	52.040	-0.018
1953.1	17.500	32983.000	15.800	52.040	2.074
1953.2	16.800	33387.600	16.600	52.010	4.695
1953.3	16.800	34606.390	15.200	52.010	1.992
1953.4	16.800	37732.000	15.000	51.850	1.349
1954.1	16.600	38787.800	14.900	51.780	0.727
1954.2	17.000	38901.600	14.500	51.890	-0.447
1954.3	17.800	40015.000	14.800	51.890	0.717
1954.4	19.100	43879.300	15.200	51.980	1.255
1955.1	19.300	45492.100	16.400	51.980	1.770
1955.2	19.600	45092.190	16.400	51.980	3.121
1955.3	19.900	46155.690	16.800	51.980	1.709
1955.4	20.400	51612.500	17.000	52.050	0.832
1956.1	20.700	53742.190	17.600	52.050	-0.030
1956.2	22.300	53278.890	17.900	52.010	-1.512
1956.3	22.900	54709.000	19.200	52.010	-0.030
1956.4	23.800	60237.890	19.500	52.090	0.572
1957.1	24.800	64035.300	20.700	52.250	1.161
1957.2	27.000	63732.190	21.900	52.400	1.360
1957.3	29.500	63596.800	24.400	52.600	1.135
1957.4	30.700	67583.500	27.800	52.650	1.505
1958.1	30.600	71933.180	29.200	52.570	1.857
1958.2	34.400	72469.000	28.600	53.180	3.703
1958.3	38.700	80185.810	32.600	53.590	1.790
1958.4	43.600	98827.310	37.500	54.300	0.243
1959.1	59.800	109052.300	43.200	54.890	-1.316
1959.2	76.200	122990.600	63.300	80.890	-4.689
1959.3	87.100	121452.600	80.800	58.970	-1.351
1959.4	91.300	103786.800	91.400	59.880	0.365

Table 4-12 (Argentina) continued

1960.3	———	162348.000	102.400	115.390	1.815
1960.4	102.600	178639.800	102.500	115.850	1.682
1961.1	103.900	184123.000	102.800	119.390	2.744
1961.2	111.400	186227.100	108.500	120.980	1.628
1961.3	117.600	187318.100	114.800	121.190	0.405
1961.4	122.300	205444.600	118.800	121.290	-0.817
1962.1	126.200	209591.000	122.000	122.090	-2.176
1962.2	139.300	210397.100	135.800	131.690	-0.831
1962.3	155.400	208733.800	154.300	131.690	-0.723
1962.4	161.900	219727.300	159.100	131.690	-0.612
1963.1	167.000	228892.500	160.700	143.290	-1.947
1963.2	176.100	240021.000	169.100	143.290	-0.620
1963.3	181.500	252155.800	174.300	143.290	0.807
1963.4	199.200	268256.100	197.800	146.690	2.180
1964.1	208.700	302421.300	211.400	146.690	3.624
1964.2	217.000	335949.800	221.100	146.690	2.089
1964.3	220.000	350429.300	219.500	146.690	1.943
1964.4	237.200	395649.300	238.500	178.090	1.803
1965.1	249.800	414087.100	246.200	184.560	1.265
1965.2	267.700	431600.100	264.200	186.690	1.741
1965.3	294.500	446037.000	299.000	186.690	2.107
1965.4	323.400	497607.600	329.800	376.190	2.449
1966.1	344.000	513902.000	351.000	376.390	3.690
1966.2	362.300	546654.600	346.900	403.390	2.334
1966.3	376.200	584998.600	394.600	416.890	1.375
1966.4	414.600	671675.300	405.700	456.300	0.447
1967.1	435.800	684200.000	426.000	456.300	-0.606
1967.2	460.100	745600.000	479.000	456.300	0.443
1967.3	500.300	741300.000	529.800	456.300	0.753
1967.4	538.500	871100.000	532.300	536.600	1.056
1968.1	552.700	889900.000	522.700	536.600	0.879
1968.2	550.800	960900.000	516.900	536.600	1.034
1968.3	555.200	996900.000	559.500	565.000	1.498
1968.4	589.800	1105000.000	554.600	565.000	1.939
1969.1	592.500	1124700.000	549.700	565.000	2.788
1969.2	591.300	1154700.000	557.100	565.000	1.867
1969.3	601.000	1172000.000	601.300	597.000	1.420
1969.4	634.200	1219100.000	601.300	597.000	1.528
1970.1	643.100	1235700.000	601.300	597.000	0.989
1970.2	661.300	1302500.000	622.900	597.000	0.557
1970.3	684.100	1319800.000	651.200	597.000	0.970
1970.4	758.500	1470200.000	760.300	597.000	0.962
1971.1	829.400	1475100.000	826.700	858.600	0.954
1971.2	874.800	1601300.000	874.700	858.600	0.827
1971.3	957.800	1693400.000	969.000	858.600	0.937
1971.4	1039.300	2002200.000	1064.200	858.600	1.048
1972.1	1252.700	2108099.000	1278.300	1068.000	1.155
1972.2	1383.600	2209699.000	1411.900	1068.000	1.149
1972.3	1523.100	2348499.000	1582.100	1068.000	1.129
1972.4	1725.200	2882400.000	1808.000	2787.290	1.228
1972.5	2094.600	4166699.000	2195.600	2844.630	1.323
1973.1	2394.500	4797499.000	2449.700	2900.890	1.310
1973.2	2680.000	5447099.000	2312.300	2900.890	1.289
1973.3	2522.100	6286800.000	2495.200	2925.000	1.380
1973.4	2746.400	5805999.000	2458.100	2925.000	1.467
1974.1	2979.700	6679999.000	2561.700	2925.000	1.553
1974.2		7389400.000	2700.500	3435.190	1.045
1974.3					**0.674**

Table 4–13
Indexes for Brazil for 1947–1974

Period	General Price Index	Money Supply	Food Price Index	Housing Price Index	Change in Real Income
1947.3	0.803	43.867	0.743	1.170	
1947.4	0.826	43.300	0.782	1.370	
1948.1	0.872	43.267	0.854	1.170	
1948.2	0.878	43.133	0.865	1.170	
1948.3	0.841	43.733	0.802	1.170	
1948.4	0.844	45.367	0.801	1.170	
1949.1	0.895	47.433	0.852	1.170	
1949.2	0.912	49.000	0.865	1.170	
1949.3	0.881	51.267	0.866	1.170	
1949.4	0.892	53.500	0.905	1.170	
1950.1	0.955	54.467	0.951	1.340	1.561
1950.2	0.970	57.200	0.934	1.407	1.548
1950.3	0.982	63.967	0.953	1.443	1.493
1950.4	1.009	69.867	0.981	1.480	1.440
1951.1	1.077	72.033	1.077	1.520	1.021
1951.2	1.080	74.633	1.130	1.607	1.400
1951.3	1.127	73.033	1.033	1.713	1.744
1951.4	1.107	82.400	1.053	1.817	2.069
1952.1	1.223	83.833	1.217	1.923	3.025
1952.2	1.277	84.767	1.283	2.020	1.987
1952.3	1.307	89.867	1.307	2.113	1.313
1952.4	1.343	94.700	1.347	2.210	0.659
1953.1	1.400	97.200	1.420	2.280	-0.929
1953.2	1.457	101.867	1.527	2.357	0.653
1953.3	1.467	105.333	1.610	2.417	1.571
1953.4	1.570	112.533	1.700	2.493	2.438
1954.1	1.650	118.967	1.833	2.690	3.583
1954.2	1.757	122.767	1.850	2.810	2.325
1954.3	1.833	131.500	2.007	2.910	1.978
1954.4	1.963	140.333	2.100	3.007	1.649
1955.1		143.433	2.213	3.100	1.717
1955.2	2.077	148.933	2.307	3.203	1.596
1955.3	2.173	155.500	2.497	3.353	1.179
1955.4	2.250	163.800	2.720	3.443	0.775
1956.1	2.373	170.367	2.737	3.590	-0.260
1956.2	2.530	180.833	2.840	3.730	-0.763
1956.3	2.593	187.700	3.013	3.900	1.380
1956.4	2.733	196.333	3.197	4.073	1.968
1957.1	2.880	204.833	3.237	4.313	2.520
1957.2	3.027	214.667	3.217	4.490	1.893
1957.3	3.127	227.533	3.353	4.623	1.885
1957.4	3.260	255.000	3.627	4.750	1.876
1958.1	3.390	277.900	3.727	4.957	2.057
1958.2	3.513	295.067	3.647	5.190	1.808
1958.3	3.583	309.500	3.907	5.430	1.589
1958.4	3.813	323.900	4.563	5.673	1.379
1959.1	4.317	337.600	5.030	5.920	0.632
1959.2	4.700	357.167	5.203	6.203	1.342
1959.3	5.147	398.600	5.513	6.493	1.856
1959.4	5.740	448.067	5.533	6.816	2.339

Table 4-13 (Brazil) continued

1960.2	6.233	510.433	6.820	7.393	2.234
1960.3	6.460	548.333	6.980	7.680	2.361
1960.4	7.083	619.400	7.597	8.030	2.478
1961.1	7.537	683.333	8.200	8.357	3.093
1961.2	8.090	727.333	8.777	8.687	1.811
1961.3	8.697	795.667	9.510	9.037	1.287
1961.4	10.010	922.000	11.500	9.417	1.189
1962.1	11.233	1017.333	13.000	11.433	1.254
1962.2	12.167	1097.000	14.200	11.899	0.817
1962.3	13.600	1255.000	16.300	12.333	0.388
1962.4	15.133	1484.666	17.967	12.900	-0.211
1963.1	17.367	1652.333	20.067	13.533	0.385
1963.2	20.267	1719.333	23.367	14.400	0.551
1963.3	23.433	1962.666	26.233	22.133	0.714
1963.4	27.600	2280.000	32.133	23.733	0.885
1964.1	33.933	2595.000	41.300	25.333	0.704
1964.2	39.800	2780.000	46.867	26.767	0.690
1964.3	45.267	3197.666	53.733	28.433	0.676
1964.4	51.133	3756.666	57.900	31.033	0.368
1965.1	60.733	4508.000	66.100	38.300	0.667
1965.2	69.133	5106.000	72.533	53.367	0.956
1965.3	73.900	5894.000	75.767	61.200	1.236
1965.4	78.133	6993.332	79.800	67.767	1.505
1966.1	86.733	8139.664	90.200	73.233	1.206
1966.2	96.467	8385.000	101.333	86.500	1.200
1966.3	104.667	8579.000	105.667	108.666	1.194
1966.4	110.667	8925.000	110.667	121.000	0.607
1967.1	119.333	9483.664	119.667	125.333	1.166
1967.2	128.000	10094.320	124.333	138.000	1.726
1967.3	134.333	11522.660	126.333	159.000	2.255
1967.4	138.333	12784.000	128.333	171.000	2.723
1968.1	145.000	13994.320	132.000	177.000	2.158
1968.2	154.667	14854.320	139.667	190.000	2.166
1968.3	163.667	16610.660	142.667	212.000	2.172
1968.4	171.000	17562.660	148.333	225.667	2.082
1969.1	179.667	19316.320	158.667	231.000	2.087
1969.2	187.667	20482.000	168.000	242.333	2.131
1969.3	198.667	21860.320	175.333	259.667	2.176
1969.4	211.667	22890.320	193.000	274.667	2.085
1970.1	220.000	25159.320	201.333	282.000	1.849
1970.2	229.667	26195.660	204.000	293.000	2.411
1970.3	244.667	28388.320	224.333	311.667	2.711
1970.4	258.000	29723.000	238.333	326.333	2.979
1971.1	267.667	33095.660	249.333	332.000	2.572
1971.2	279.000	35844.320	261.000	340.667	2.537
1971.3	293.000	39223.660	272.667	363.000	2.503
1971.4	304.000	43454.660	283.333	380.667	2.235
1972.1	317.300	43688.660	298.667	372.333	2.383
1972.2	327.667	47353.320	305.667	379.667	2.561
1972.3	340.000	50321.320	319.333	397.667	2.723
1972.4	348.333	57069.320	331.000	403.000	2.668
1973.1	358.333	60417.320	342.000	405.667	2.583
1973.2	370.667	69267.310	354.667	416.333	2.734
1973.3	379.667	76201.000	362.667	428.000	2.871
1973.4	393.000	85936.620	380.667	433.000	3.096
1974.1	426.000	90524.310	428.667	446.330	2.715
1974.2	471.000	97510.310	488.000	489.000	2.557
1974.3	497.333	101868.300	512.667	515.670	

Table 4-14
Indexes for Chile for 1935-1974

Period	General Price Index	Money Supply	Food Price Index	Change in Real Income
1938.1	0.089	1.949	0.112	
1938.2	0.093	2.018	0.120	
1938.3	0.093	1.831	0.117	
1938.4	0.094	1.941	0.118	
1939.1	0.089	2.209	0.108	
1939.2	0.094	2.362	0.114	
1939.3	0.094	2.303	0.113	
1939.4	0.098	2.374	0.123	
1940.1	0.098	2.697	0.124	0.027
1940.2	0.104	2.875	0.132	0.015
1940.3	0.109	2.714	0.136	0.022
1940.4	0.111	2.764	0.141	-0.003
1941.1	0.110	3.064	0.133	-0.029
1941.2	0.118	3.191	0.146	-0.003
1941.3	0.125	3.014	0.160	0.005
1941.4	0.132	3.190	0.172	0.013
1942.1	0.138	3.725	0.177	0.022
1942.2	0.151	3.969	0.193	0.012
1942.3	0.156	3.740	0.206	0.011
1942.4	0.166	3.993	0.223	0.009
1943.1	0.167	4.922	0.221	0.011
1943.2	0.180	5.240	0.242	0.009
1943.3	0.181	5.408	0.243	0.006
1943.4	0.182	5.517	0.239	0.004
1944.1	0.183	5.886	0.238	-0.010
1944.2	0.194	6.087	0.242	0.004
1944.3	0.202	6.112	0.255	0.014
1944.4	0.215	6.221	0.278	0.023
1945.1	0.207	6.509	0.255	0.037
1945.2	0.212	6.744	0.262	0.022
1945.3	0.218	6.870	0.274	0.018
1945.4	0.225	7.243	0.287	0.014
1946.1	0.225	7.741	0.283	0.025
1946.2	0.237	8.230	0.295	0.013
1946.3	0.257	8.675	0.322	-0.002
1946.4	0.281	9.195	0.355	-0.017
1947.1	0.308	9.572	0.400	-0.059
1947.2	0.329	10.451	0.407	-0.018

Table 4-14 (Chile) continued

Period	General Price Index	Money Supply	Food Price Index	Change in Real Income
1947.3	0.346	10.436	0.431	0.007
1947.4	0.354	10.853	0.443	0.002
1948.1	0.368	11.963	0.460	0.065
1948.2	0.384	12.948	0.473	0.028
1948.3	0.407	14.311	0.509	0.015
1948.4	0.418	15.289	0.514	0.002
1949.1	0.431	16.388	0.531	-0.017
1949.2	0.462	17.261	0.547	0.002
1949.3	0.477	17.685	0.566	0.007
1949.4	0.502	18.664	0.606	0.013
1950.1	0.502	18.920	0.600	0.017
1950.2	0.519	18.875	0.610	0.012
1950.3	0.543	19.013	0.656	0.013
1950.4	0.593	19.452	0.760	0.013
1951.1	0.595	21.415	0.732	0.011
1951.2	0.621	24.192	0.751	0.013
1951.3	0.692	24.249	0.878	0.015
1951.4	0.728	26.049	0.945	0.017
1952.1	0.733	27.875	0.943	0.019
1952.2	0.791	30.642	1.044	0.016
1952.3	0.847	32.818	1.131	0.016
1952.4	0.851	33.988	1.109	0.016
1953.1	0.852	37.675	1.034	0.025
1953.2	0.890	43.355	1.073	0.016
1953.3	1.056	44.814	1.355	0.007
1953.4	1.240	49.237	1.687	-0.002
1954.1	1.369	57.071	1.837	-0.012
1954.2	1.608	64.141	2.173	-0.002
1954.3	1.868	66.570	2.621	0.000
1954.4	2.108	73.459	2.962	0.002
1955.1	2.355	82.032	3.307	0.004
1955.2	2.839	96.942	3.800	0.002
1955.3	3.193	101.716	4.191	0.002
1955.4	3.797	110.104	4.676	0.003
1956.1	4.168	121.084	5.481	-0.007
1956.2	4.416	141.449	5.538	0.002
1956.3	4.923	146.820	6.608	0.012
1956.4	5.494	156.125	7.826	0.021
1957.1	5.522	175.007	7.552	0.037
1957.2	6.065	188.823	8.575	0.020
1957.3	7.039	195.319	10.613	0.012
1957.4	6.681	200.588	9.248	0.004
1958.1	6.830	219.792	8.908	-0.000
1958.2	7.392	230.445	9.512	0.004
1958.3	7.797	253.085	9.799	0.001
1958.4	8.349	270.106	10.512	-0.002
1959.1	9.191	295.728	11.397	-0.012
1959.2	10.262	317.694	12.846	-0.002
1959.3	11.178	326.162	14.444	0.006
1959.4	11.469	323.223	14.963	0.014
1960.1	11.524	341.148	14.986	0.021
1960.2	11.492	360.331	14.708	0.014
1960.3	11.919	407.727	15.803	0.014
1960.4	12.040	447.878	16.032	0.015
1961.1	12.233	480.002	16.342	0.016
1961.2	12.446	489.009	16.468	0.014
1961.3	12.607	476.752	17.136	0.014
1961.4	13.093	499.087	17.733	0.013
1962.1	13.435	555.093	18.291	0.014
1962.2	13.696	572.695	18.462	0.013
1962.3	14.247	575.804	19.479	0.012
1962.4	16.239	652.482	22.994	0.010
1963.1	18.132	777.244	25.292	0.008

Table 4-14 (Chile) continued

Period	General Price Index	Money Supply	Food Price Index	Change in Real Income
1963.2	19.878	852.359	27.710	0.010
1963.3	21.541	848.740	30.882	0.011
1963.4	23.550	918.140	34.817	0.011
1964.1	26.711	1008.000	39.316	0.004
1964.2	29.578	1175.660	42.841	0.011
1964.3	31.600	1249.560	46.514	0.019
1964.4	33.419	1334.460	49.716	0.026
1965.1	35.001	1598.600	51.362	0.034
1965.2	39.025	1745.860	58.140	0.025
1965.3	40.222	1911.800	59.302	0.023
1965.4	42.046	2106.760	62.365	0.022
1966.1	44.678	2269.230	66.603	0.029
1966.2	47.052	2613.600	68.255	0.021
1966.3	49.916	2803.130	74.314	0.012
1966.4	50.400	2960.930	73.952	0.002
1967.1	52.186	3112.030	75.240	-0.010
1967.2	55.585	3269.260	78.907	0.002
1967.3	58.728	3264.330	83.961	0.006
1967.4	60.386	3459.500	85.950	0.009
1968.1	65.346	3929.300	93.309	0.010
1968.2	69.972	4278.559	97.334	0.009
1968.3	74.765	4602.500	106.487	0.011
1968.4	77.222	5074.727	109.563	0.013
1969.1	84.925	5763.457	120.786	0.017
1969.2	93.193	6306.699	131.698	0.013
1969.3	97.722	6308.059	138.938	0.012
1969.4	99.529	7018.199	140.145	0.010
1970.1	111.730	8249.430	112.707	0.006
1970.2	121.450	9298.699	123.770	0.010
1970.3	129.570	10091.820	135.473	0.013
1970.4	134.650	11273.390	140.527	0.016
1971.1	138.063	14710.250	144.110	0.027

Table 4–15

Indexes for Mexico for 1947–1974

Period	General Price Index	Money Supply	Food Price Index	Change in Real Income
1947.3	63.163	3358.003	64.588	
1947.4	63.179	3449.875	64.644	
1948.1	63.187	3458.601	63.560	
1948.2	65.327	3535.018	66.133	
1948.3	67.111	3690.489	67.129	
1948.4	66.449	3851.859	65.496	
1949.1	65.666	3951.341	63.608	
1949.2	67.853	3929.479	66.898	
1949.3	69.565	4069.613	68.554	
1949.4	69.694	4265.230	67.463	
1950.1	68.653	4499.020	65.504	3.124
1950.2	72.479	4555.637	70.084	2.275
1950.3	74.296	5064.074	71.278	1.979
1950.4	77.969	5706.754	74.305	1.698
1951.1	83.192	6412.504	79.936	1.813
1951.2	91.790	6194.609	90.968	1.802
1951.3	95.092	6340.125	96.033	1.374
1951.4	95.116	6662.484	95.954	0.957
1952.1	95.367	6665.328	96.067	0.987
1952.2	98.267	6344.129	100.367	0.941
1952.3	96.067	6345.063	97.633	0.492
1952.4	94.600	6818.668	95.467	0.050
1953.1	90.967	7120.031	90.800	-1.689
1953.2	93.067	7045.133	94.333	0.048
1953.3	94.767	7080.332	96.867	1.318
1953.4	94.567	7422.930	96.767	2.524
1954.1	93.767	7609.133	95.100	3.793
1954.2	99.800	7365.500	101.200	2.401
1954.3	101.667	7812.066	100.600	2.256
1954.4	104.733	8378.199	103.100	2.119
1955.1	108.300	8887.500	107.400	2.159
1955.2	113.100	9178.832	112.800	2.033
1955.3	117.667	9604.531	117.167	1.815
1955.4	119.800	10096.550	119.133	1.610
1956.1	120.967	10448.080	121.033	1.235
1956.2	122.167	10262.620	122.400	1.560
1956.3	120.733	10506.820	120.067	1.705
1956.4	119.933	11192.820	118.500	1.844
1957.1	121.867	11376.030	120.900	2.169
1957.2	125.800	11317.000	126.433	1.778
1957.3	130.300	11608.500	132.233	1.558
1957.4	128.400	12012.550	128.800	1.347
1958.1	130.267	12225.420	131.633	1.427
1958.2	135.100	12071.620	138.033	1.312
1958.3	134.400	12277.620	136.633	1.008
1958.4	135.067	12842.190	137.467	0.713
1959.1	135.967	13231.760	138.400	0.244
1959.2	135.200	13580.780	137.333	0.702
1959.3	134.833	14008.280	136.833	0.873
1959.4	132.700	14677.120	133.566	1.037
1960.1	134.066	15091.120	135.000	1.089
1960.2	140.100	15283.960	143.533	1.015

Table 4-15 (Mexico) continued

Period	General Price Index	Money Supply	Food Price Index	Change in Real Income
1960.3	143.767	15537.030	148.433	1.115
1960.4	141.100	16245.320	144.267	1.211
1961.1	140.233	16490.760	142.933	1.311
1961.2	141.267	16276.850	143.467	1.182
1961.3	141.467	16261.500	143.567	1.163
1961.4	141.367	17115.350	141.667	1.146
1962.1	142.467	17446.280	143.400	0.690
1962.2	145.800	17268.980	147.333	1.120
1962.3	147.533	17726.960	149.767	1.541
1962.4	146.566	18998.580	148.600	1.940
1963.1	144.967	19684.690	146.167	1.812
1963.2	145.833	19695.920	147.267	1.869
1963.3	145.333	20238.620	146.566	2.352
1963.4	144.567	22101.390	145.600	2.801
1964.1	149.066	23480.160	152.000	3.724
1964.2	151.267	23608.120	154.533	2.652
1964.3	153.667	24533.350	157.200	2.102
1964.4	153.500	26250.050	156.667	1.582
1965.1	153.400	26788.620	155.933	0.959
1965.2	155.566	26373.550	157.933	1.533
1965.3	156.467	26048.350	158.833	1.614
1965.4	156.000	27633.500	158.100	1.690
1966.1	155.667	28665.140	157.533	1.794
1966.2	156.467	28336.890	158.700	1.634
1966.3	160.333	28360.120	163.200	1.582
1966.4	160.933	30334.160	163.700	1.530
1967.1	162.867	31232.440	166.367	1.204
1967.2	163.033	30890.280	165.900	1.485
1967.3	165.400	31003.710	168.767	1.737
1967.4	166.333	32858.510	170.100	1.975
1968.1	165.767	34030.460	169.100	2.357
1968.2	168.667	34172.460	173.233	1.900
1968.3	169.567	34428.570	173.733	1.717
1968.4	168.433	36958.660	171.066	1.543
1969.1	168.867	37548.410	170.300	1.250
1969.2	169.767	37704.750	171.533	1.497
1969.3	175.000	37807.620	179.100	1.594
1969.4	178.033	40508.570	183.433	1.689
1970.1	178.300	41609.350	183.233	2.153
1970.2	186.500	41421.820	189.700	1.633
1970.3	189.566	41527.010	193.600	1.234
1970.4	186.967	44990.960	189.767	0.849
1971.1	189.967	44993.960	193.367	-0.028
1971.2	194.500	44716.780	197.267	0.834
1971.3	196.500	44628.250	201.500	1.312
1971.4	194.767	48191.190	198.967	1.769
1972.1	195.333	50446.320	199.633	2.121
1972.2	199.433	50347.160	203.667	1.709
1972.3	201.967	51911.510	206.267	1.779
1972.4	203.067	57827.370	206.267	1.846
1973.1	211.000	61484.030	214.367	2.050
1973.2	221.967	63192.250	227.867	1.780
1973.3	236.100	65478.670	243.267	1.611
1973.4	248.967	72879.680	256.800	1.450
1974.1	271.700	75071.680	282.470	1.499
1974.2	282.500	77051.120	293.300	1.409
1974.3	288.830	78510.120	299.670	1.183

5 Summary

Inflation has plagued Latin America since the late Nineteenth Century. Two competing schools of thought, monetarism and structuralism, have developed in Latin America to explain chronic inflation. These hypotheses are examined and tested here, using data from Argentina, Chile, Brazil, and Mexico. Latin American monetarism suggests that the factors which cause inflation in Latin America are similar to those causing inflation elsewhere and are primarily a matter of excess demand. Latin American structuralism, however, stresses that there are factors peculiar to Latin America's institutional structure which explain why that region is predisposed to inflation. Specifically, according to the structuralist view, the relative backwardness of agriculture in many of Latin America's inflationary economies explains that region's propensity toward inflation. Structuralists argue that inflation results because agricultural prices rise over time. Since other prices do not fall, the price level increases. The downward rigidity in nonfood prices is ascribed to the pervasiveness of imperfect competition in the manufacturing and service sectors. The structuralist explanation of inflation is criticized here on empirical and theoretical grounds. First, historically, in Latin American inflationary economies, when excess supply exists in manufacturing and service sectors, prices are not merely rigid downwards in these sectors; rather, they continue to rise. Second, for this argument alone to explain why inflation increases over time, as it has in several Latin American economies, the relative price of food would not only have to rise; it would have to rise at an ever-increasing rate. This has not occurred in those Latin American economies with a secularly rising inflation rate. Third, structuralism does not provide a theoretical justification for the assumed downward rigidity of nonfood prices. Fourth, structuralists do not grant any causal role to demand-pull or expectational factors in their framework. The money supply is regarded as increasing in response to a rising price level but not as initiating price increases. Finally, the testable implications of the structuralist hypothesis, as traditionally stated, are not clear. The structuralist argument is reformulated here to deal with these criticisms. In the reformulated model it is not argued that there is a floor to downward price movements outside of agriculture. Rather, it is assumed that agricultural prices adjust more rapidly to excess demand or to excess supply than do prices elsewhere. That is, food prices are assumed to be more flexible than nonfood prices.

A suggested explanation for the slower adjustment of prices outside of agriculture is the interest of oligopolies in these sectors in preserving an industry-wide pricing structure. Then, if prices rise in agriculture, even if aggregate demand is not excessive, inflation results in the short run. This comes about as follows: If excess demand prevails in agriculture, balanced by an equivalent amount of excess supply elsewhere, agricultural prices will rise in response to the excess demand in that sector, but prices outside of agriculture will not fall an equivalent amount. A short-run rise in the price level has occurred, along with a rise in the relative price of food. If aggregate demand is excessive, prices will rise for this reason, but they will rise more, and again a rise in the relative price of food will occur if excess demand is concentrated in agriculture. Furthermore, once inflation becomes anticipated and these expectations are validated by monetary and fiscal policy, an ongoing inflation is possible at the equilibrium-expected rate. Then, the existence of excess demand in agriculture, balanced by excess supply elsewhere, will lead to a rise in the inflation rate. However, the higher inflation rate cannot persist in the long run without changes in government policy. As prices rise, real balances fall if the rate of monetary expansion is not increased. The decline in real balances will eventually slow the inflation rate since the velocity of money cannot increase without bounds. Thus, for the higher inflation rate to be maintained, money must respond; but it is quite possible that the money supply is passive and does respond to higher prices. Fiscal and monetary authorities may increase the money supply as prices rise in an effort to prevent the increased unemployment, higher interest rates, and lowered government real purchasing power that would otherwise result. Finally, to confirm the structuralist position, the relative price of food must rise over time. Falling relative food prices would result in less inflation.

The reformulated structuralist model developed here can be compared to Schultze's model of structural imbalances. Inflation occurs in both models in the absence of excess aggregate demand due to the existence of structural imbalances. However, in Schultze's model, price reaction coefficients are the same across sectors, and inflation results in the absence of excess aggregate demand, because prices in all sectors react more quickly to excess demand than to excess supply.

The Latin American monetarist and the reformulated structuralist models are tested by estimating inflation equations which include demand-pull and expectational variables as well as a variable which reflects the concentration of excess demand in agriculture. Harberger's model of inflation provides one measure of the strength of excess aggregate demand factors. In Harberger's model, inflation is the result of an excess supply of money. The rate of change in the demand for money at a given inflation rate is determined by the rate of growth of real income and the change in the cost of holding money. The rate of change in the money supply is determined by monetary and fiscal authorities. The inflation rate adjusts to equate the demand for money to the supply and is thus a function of the rate of change in real income and in the cost of holding money and the rate of monetary expansion. Alternatively, the strength of demand-pull factors can be reflected in the Phillips-curve approach in the level of the unemployment rate at a given expected inflation rate. These models of inflation, both of which conform to the Latin American monetarist view of inflation, are augmented to include the rate of change in the relative price of food. This variable reflects the extent to which aggregate demand is concentrated in the agriculture sector since, for a given level of excess aggregate demand, the greater the concentration of excess demand in agriculture, the greater the rise in the relative price of food.

The empirical results of the study support a broad model of inflation. The findings of significant coefficients with the anticipated signs for the demand-pull and expectational variables in the Harberger and Phillips-curve equations are consistent with the Latin American monetarist argument that excessive aggregate demand is responsible for inflation. However, the reformulated structuralist model is also substantially supported by the finding, in the equations using quarterly data, of a significant and positive coefficient for the rate of change in the relative price of food.

The possible long-run impact of structural inflation is tested, using a technique developed by Sims. The Sims procedure tests for the existence of a passive money supply in a two-way regression between prices and money. The outcome of these tests suggests that the structuralist hypothesis of a passive money supply cannot be rejected for Brazil, Chile, or Mexico. Therefore, these results, taken together, support a broad model in which inflation in these economies depends on the concentration of excess demand in agriculture as well as on the overall level of excess aggregate demand. A finding of passive money in Argentina is not supported by this test. This may reflect stop-go economic policies pursued in Argentina in this period, or an omission of variables in the Sims test. The results of the Harberger test indicate that structural imbalances have an impact on the Argentinian inflation rate, in the short run. If, as implied in the Sims test, monetary authorities do not consistently ratify structural inflation, this impact does not result in a permanently higher rate of inflation, in spite of the secular rise in relative food prices in Argentina, over this period. Rather, real income is likely to be affected.

Finally, since the relative price of food in Chile and Brazil has increased over time, this suggests that the rate of change in the relative price of food has been positive more often than negative and, therefore, that the inflation rate in these Latin American economies has been higher than would have been the case if purely monetarist variables were at work. The fall in relative food prices in Mexico in this period suggests that the strength of the agriculture sector has contributed to this economy's relatively low inflation rate. In attempting to control inflation, these results imply that policies that improve agricultural productivity, along with the traditional policies of controlling excess aggregate demand, will aid in limiting the inflationary process.

Notes

Notes

Preface

1. Roberto Campos, "Two Views on Inflation in Latin America," *Latin American Issues* A.O. Hirschman, ed. (New York: Twentieth Century Fund, 1961), pp. 69-73

2. Arnold Harberger, "The Dynamics of Inflation in Chile," in *Measurement in Economics: Studies in Mathematical Economics in Memory of Yehuda Grunfeld* Carl Carl Christ, ed., (Stanford: Stanford University Press, 1963), pp. 219-250.

3. See Dudley Seers, "A Theory of Inflation and Growth in Underdeveloped Economies based on the Experience of Latin America," *Oxford Economic Papers*, 1962, XIV, No. 2; Raul Prebisch, "Structural Vulnerability and Inflation," *Leading Issues in Economic Development: Studies in International Poverty*, 1970, pp. 238-241; and, Osvaldo Sunkel, "Inflation in Chile: An Unorthodox Approach," *International Economic Papers*, No. 10.

4. Jorge Cauas, "Stabilization Policy – The Chilean Case," *Journal of Political Economy*, July–August 1970, p. 816.

Chapter 1
The Latin American Monetarist-Structuralist Debate

1. There are variations in the monetarist position. Those most often used are summarized here. A more extensive summary of the monetarist postion is presented in Roberto Campos, "Two Views on Inflation in Latin America," A.O. Hirschman, ed., *Latin American Issues* (New York: Twentieth Century Fund, 1961), pp. 69-73.

2. Arnold Harberger, "The Dynamics of Inflation in Chile," in *Measurement in Economics: Studies in Mathematical Economics in Memory of Yehuda Grunfeld* Carl Christ, ed., (Stanford: Stanford University Press, 1963), pp. 219-250.

3. There are many variations in the structuralist approach. Those that are used most frequently are summarized here. Dudley Seers, "A Theory of Inflation and Growth in Underdeveloped Economies based on the Experience of Latin America," *Oxford Economic Papers*, XIV, No. 2 (1962),

examines in his appendix the contribution that various economists have made to the theory.

4. Leopoldo Solis, "Mexican Economic Policy in the Post-War Period: The Views of Mexican Economists," *American Economic Review*, June 1971, p. 34.

5. Albert Hirschman, "Inflation in Chile," in *Journeys Toward Progress* (New York: Twentieth Century Fund, 1963), pp. 159–226. The Klein-Saks stabilization mission, named after the foreign experts who were invited to advise the Chilean government on how to slow inflation, suggested, among other reforms, a slowing of the growth of the money supply and a freeing of exchange rates and other controlled prices. Beginning in 1955 when the reforms were implemented, the rate of monetary expansion, in fact, did drop, from an annual rate of 65% in 1955, to 40% in 1956, and to 28% in 1957. The inflation rate also declined, from 84% in 1955, to 38% in 1956, and to 17% in 1957. However, the unemployment and stagnation that accompanied the lower inflation led to the abandonment of the stabilization efforts in 1958.

6. Some structuralists, as described below, see government policy which favors industry at the expense of agriculture as also responsible for the secular rise in relative food prices.

7. Refer to bibliography for citations. The following section represents a summary of the work of these economists.

8. As shown in "Aggregative Market Response in Developing Agriculture: The Postwar Chilean Experience" by Jere Behrman, Chapter 2 in *Analysis of Development Problems: Studies of Chilean Economy*, Richard Eckaus, and Paul N. Rosenstein-Rodan, eds. (Amsterdam: North-Holland, 1973), pp. 229–250, the agriculture sector in Chile is not unresponsive to economic signals. The explanation for low land productivity is, thus, obviously a complicated one. Theodore Schultz, *Transforming Traditional Agriculture* (New Haven: Yale University Press, 1964), argues that the missing factor is public infrastructure investment. It may be that the holders of land in Chile do not demand such an infrastructure and the increase in taxes that would go with it. The desire for bringing the government into the promotion of agricultural growth in this way may be correlated with the rural class structure so that, for example, the Mexican Revolution brought a new class of landowners who sought more growth and more government involvement in agriculture.

9. Seers, "A Theory of Inflation and Growth," p. 183.

10. Joseph Grunwald, "The 'Structuralist' School on Price Stability and Development: The Chilean Case" in *Latin American Issues* Albert O. Hirschman, ed., (New York: Twentieth Century Fund, 1961), pp. 110–111.

11. Geoffrey Maynard, "Inflation and Growth: Some Lessons to be Drawn

from Latin American Experience," *Oxford Economic Papers,* June 1961. A discussion of the effect government policy has had on growth in agriculture is not possible here. There is evidence in Ian Little, Tibor Scitovsky, and Maurice Scott, *Industry and Trade in Some Developing Countries* (London: Oxford University Press, 1970) that in several Latin American countries government had a significant negative impact.

12. Maynard, "Inflation and Growth: Some Lessons," p. 202.

13. Ibid., p. 202.

14. David Felix, "An Alternative View of the Monetarist-Structuralist Controversy," in A.O. Hirschman, ed., *Latin American Issues* (New York: Twentieth Century Fund, 1961), p. 86.

15. W. A. Lewis, "Economic Development with Unlimited Supplies of Labour," *The Manchester School,* May 1954.

16. J. Harris and M. Todaro, "Migration, Unemployment, and Development: A Two Sector Analysis," *American Economic Review,* March 1970.

17. Seers, "A Theory of Inflation and Growth."

18. Ibid., p. 182.

19. It has been suggested that this is a more important explanation for exchange rate deterioration, see Irving Kravis, "Trade as a Handmaiden of Growth: Similarities Between the 19th and 20th Centuries," University of Pennsylvania, Department of Economics, Discussion Paper No. 105, 1968, and Carlos F. Diaz-Alejandro, *Essays on the Economic History of the Argentine Republic* (New Haven: Yale University Press, 1970).

20. Maynard, "Inflation and Growth: Some Lessons," p. 197.

21. Julio H. G. Olivera, "On Structural Inflation and Latin American 'Structuralism,'" *Oxford Economic Papers,* November 1964, p. 325. Latin American structuralist theory shares this assumption with Schultze's theory of sectoral imbalances. Similarities in the two theories are discussed further in Section V. This assumption is also used in the Latin American inflation literature by those who are not in the structuralist school. For example, Diaz-Alejandro attributes Argentinian inflation, in part, to this. "In an economy where downward price flexibility is limited, attempts to change relative prices will lead to an upward movement in the price level. The price structure may be changed, but only in the context of a rising price level." (Diaz-Alejandro, p. 121.)

22. Susan H. Cochrane, "Structural Inflation and the Two-Gap Model of Economic Development," *Oxford Economic Papers,* November 1972, p. 396.

23. Werner Baer, "The Inflation Controversy in Latin America: A Survey," *Latin American Research Review,* Spring 1967, p. 8.

24. Pierre Uri with Nicholas Kaldor, Richard Ruggles, and Robert Triffin, *A Monetary Policy for Latin America* (New York: Praeger, 1968), p. 85.

25. See S. Ross and M. Wachter, "The Pricing and Timing Decision of the Oligopoly Firm," *Quarterly Journal of Economics*, February 1975.

26. It has been suggested by some structuralists, see M.W. Mueller, "Structural Inflation and the Mexican Experience," *Yale Economic Essays* E, No. 1 (Spring 1965), p. 153, P. Uri with N. Kaldor, R. Ruggles, and R. Triffin, *A Monetary Policy for Latin America* (New York: Praeger, 1968), p. 83, and D. Seers, "A Theory of Inflation and Growth in Underdeveloped Economies based on the Experience of Latin America," *Oxford Economic Papers* XIV, No. 2 (1962), p. 189, that the fact that when monetary authorities restrict the growth in credit, the decline in inflation which occurs is accompanied by a decline in economic growth disproves the neoclassical monetarist theory. Once expectations are included in an inflation model, however, it is clear that prices would not adjust immediately to a decline in aggregate demand, and that output would fall as well.

27. Alain Enthoven, "Monetary Disequilibria and the Dynamics of Inflation," *The Economic Journal*, June 1956.

28. Ibid.

29. Christopher Sims, "Money, Income, and Causality," *American Economic Review* (September 1972).

30. Charles Schultze, *Recent Inflation in the United States,* Study Paper No. 1 for the Joint Economic Committee of Congress, Washington, 1959.

31. Ibid., p. 45.

32. Ibid., p. 54.

33. In models similar to that of Schultze, James Tobin, "Inflation and Unemployment," *American Economic Review*, March 1972, and G.C. Archibald, "The Structure of Excess Demand for Labor," in Edmund Phelps, et al., *Microeconomic Foundations of Employment and Inflation Theory* (New York: W. W. Norton, 1970), pp. 212-223, also assume differing reaction speeds depending on the direction of price change and draw out this implication of the assumption. Their models are discussed further in Chapter 3.

Chapter 2
Review of Empirical Literature

1. Geoffrey Maynard, "Inflation and Growth: Some Lessons to be Drawn from Latin American Experience," *Oxford Economic Papers*, June 1961.

2. Marnie W. Mueller, "Structural Inflation and the Mexican Experience," *Yale Economic Essays*, Spring 1965.

3. Ibid., p. 157.

4. Matthew Edel, *Food Supply and Inflation in Latin America* (New York: Praeger, 1969).

5. Ibid., p. 65.
6. Arnold Harberger, "The Dynamics of Inflation in Chile," in *Measurement in Economics: Studies in Mathematical Economics in Memory of Yehuda Grunfeld*, Carl Christ, ed., (Stanford: Stanford University Press, 1963), pp. 219-250.
7. Ibid., p. 230. Harberger does not provide the Durbin-Watson statistics for his regressions. He comments on this (p. 250): "No statistical tests for serial correlation of residuals were made, but the plotted residuals were examined for evidence of serial correlation. There was no apparent serial correlation in any of the residual series." As part of the empirical testing of the monetarist and structuralist hypotheses, Harberger's equations are reestimated in Chapter 4 and the Durbin-Watson statistics are reported.
8. Harberger, "The Dynamics," p. 231.
9. Ibid., p. 235.
10. Ibid., p. 235.
11. Ibid., p. 245.
12. Ibid., pp. 247-248.
13. Ibid., p. 245.
14. See Maynard and Rijckeghem, "Stabilization Policy in an Inflationary Economy," in Papanek, ed., *Development Policy: Theory and Practice* (Cambridge: Harvard University Press, 1968), pp. 207-238.
15. See Adolfo Diz, "Money and Prices in Argentina," in *Varieties of Monetary Experience*, David Meiselman, ed. (Chicago: University of Chicago Press, 1970).
16. Ibid., p. 117.
17. Ibid., p. 120.
18. See Carlos F. Diaz-Alejandro, *Essays on the Economic History of the Argentine Republic* (New Haven: Yale University Press, 1970), pp. 366-390.
19. Ibid., p. 373.
20. Ibid., pp. 373-374.
21. See Robert Vogel, "The Dynamics of Inflation in Latin America," *American Economic Review*, March 1974.
22. Ibid., p. 107.
23. Vogel, "The Dynamics," p. 113. It is also true, as Vogel notes, that the significance of the coefficients of lagged price variables, included to reflect inflationary expectations, may actually reflect the importance of missing variables, as well as the importance of additional lags on other included independent variables. This issue is discussed further in Chapter 4.
24. Dean S. Dutton, in "A Model of Self-Generating Inflation," *Journal of Money, Credit, and Banking*, May 1971, attempts to test for the existence of passive money supply in Argentina. Dutton assumes that due to a rigid tax structure, as the inflation rate grows the real value of taxes declines and because the real value of government expenditure is fixed, the deficit grows.

Thus the deficit, and the money supply which must be printed to finance it, are a function of the inflation rate. A "rigid" tax structure and a growing deficit as inflation grows are exactly what one would expect in the case of an inflation arising from the structuralist sources described above, if monetary authorities validate the inflation. That is, his results, which support his hypothesis are also consistent with other models in which money supply is passively increasing in response to growing inflationary pressures from non-monetarist sources. However, Dutton tests only for the influence of prices on money. He does not permit reverse causality. In the Sims approach explained and used in Chapter 4, causality running in both directions is allowed. This provides a more rigorous test for the existence of passive money. For example, whereas one might find a relationship between past prices and the current money supply in the equation which Dutton estimates, $M_t = f(P_t, P_{t-1} \ldots P_{t-n})$, the same relationship might not appear if one estimated $M_t = f(P_{t+n}, \ldots, P_t, \ldots P_{t-n})$ as Sims does, allowing causality in both directions. The approach followed in Chapter 4 is an expansion of the second type of methodology.

25.   Christopher Sims, "Money, Income, and Causality," *American Economic Review*, September 1972.
26.   Ronald S. Koot, "A Test for Demand-Pull of Wage-Push Inflation: The Chilean Case," *Social and Economic Studies,* June 1968.

Chapter 3
Alternative Demand-Pull Approaches and Testable Implications
of the Structuralist and Monetarist Models

1.   Arnold Harberger, "The Dynamics of Inflation in Chile," in *Measurement in Economics: Studies in Mathematical Economics in Memory of Yehuda Grunfeld,* Carl Christ, ed., (Stanford: Stanford University Press, 1963), pp. 219-250.
2.   See P. Cagan, "The Monetary Dynamics of Hyperinflation," in Friedman, ed., *Studies in the Quantity Theory of Money* (Chicago: University of Chicago Press, 1956), pp. 25-120; Diz, "Money and Prices in Argentina"; John Deaver, "The Chilean Inflation and the Demand for Money," in David Meiselman, ed., *Varieties of Monetary Experience* (Chicago: University of Chicago Press, 1970); Dutton, "A Model of Self-Generating Inflation"; and Thomas Reichmann, "Persistent Inflation and Macroeconomic Equilibrium, The Case of Chile: 1960-1969," unpublished Ph.D. dissertation, Harvard University, 1973.
3.   Martin Bailey, *National Income and the Price Level* (New York: McGraw-Hill Book Co., 1962).

4. Thus, Y_f is defined as that level of income which in the absence of structural inflation assures that inflation will continue at its anticipated rate. If there are no inflationary expectations, $Y = Y_f$ assures zero inflation, again in the absence of structural inflation. The GNP gap $(Y_f - Y)$ reflects the deviation of the actual unemployment rate, U, from the full-employment-unemployment rate, U_f, where U_f is defined as the zero-inflation-unemployment rate in the absence of inflationary expectations and structural inflation. Note that U_f is not Keynesian full-employment at which all sectors are at full employment and no further increase in output are possible. Rather, U_f is consistent with M. Friedman's natural rate of unemployment discussed in "The Role of Monetary Policy," *American Economic Review*, March 1968. See pages 63-65 for further discussion of U_f. Assuming that U_f is not changing over time, the GNP gap and $U - U_f$ will vary with U, the actual unemployment rate.

5. Bailey, *National Income,* p. 50.

6. See, for example, G. C. Archibald, "The Structure of Excess Demand for Labor," in *Microeconomic Foundations of Employment and Inflation Theory,* pp. 212-223, edited by Edmund Phelps, et al., New York: W. W. Norton, 1970; James Tobin, "Inflation and Unemployment," *American Economic Review* (March 1972), pp. 1-18; and Robert J. Barro and Herschel I. Grossman, "A General Disequilibrium Model of Income and Employment," *American Economic Review,* (March 1971), pp. 82-93.

7. Tobin, "Inflation and Unemployment," and Archibald, "Structure of Excess Demand for Labor," also consider the relationship between the level of the dispersion of unemployment across sectors and the Phillips curve. Tobin assumes an asymmetry in the speed of price reactions depending on the direction of price movements. Prices are assumed to be more flexible upward. Thus a greater variance of unemployment rates across sectors shifts the Phillips curve out. Archibald presents evidence on this issue. Barro and Grossman, "A General Disequilibrium Model," point out that such an assumption is unnecessary for the derivation of a short-run Phillips curve relationship.

8. See M. Friedman's, "The Role of Monetary Policy," and several articles in Edmund Phelps, ed., *Inflation Policy and Unemployment Theory* (New York: W. W. Norton, 1972) for alternate theories behind the derivation of a Phillips curve. These alternate theories, to a large extent, revolve around the idea that, as inflation increases, workers will be "fooled" into thinking that the money wages offered to them are increasing faster than overall prices or others' money wages. Therefore, they will be induced into taking jobs they otherwise would not accept. This mechanism behind the short-run Phillips curve and the one outlined above are not mutually exclusive. For a review of various explanations that have been offered for the Phillips curve, see Robert J. Gordon, "Recent Developments in the

Theory of Inflation and Unemployment," presented at the International
Economics Association Conference, Sweden, August, 1975.

9.   That is, in the long run, the Phillips curve is vertical at U_f. Inflation will
     continue to spiral upward if unemployment is maintained below U_f. For
     a more comprehensive discussion of the derivation of a short-run Phillips
     curve in the presence of sectoral imbalances and of the long-run vertical
     Phillips curve, see M. Wachter and S. Wachter, "Money Wage Inflation:
     The Endogeneity-Exogeneity Issue," in Sidney Weintraub, ed., *Some
     Trends in Modern Economic Thought*, (Philadelphia: University of
     Pennsylvania Press, forthcoming, 1976.)

10. Here, too, as in the estimation of a Phillips-curve equation there is some
     degree of misspecification. Again, the misspecification takes the form
     of income being determined simultaneously with the inflation rate by
     monetary policy rather than being exogenous as assumed by Harberger.
     To get around this problem, a variable which reflects the slowly changing
     full-employment level of income rather than the actual level of income
     can be included in the Harberger equation. Furthermore, it has been
     argued by some that the demand for money may depend more on such a
     variable than on actual income. See various tests of the "permanent
     income" hypothesis in David Meiselman ed., *Varieties of Monetary
     Experience* (Chicago: University of Chicago Press, 1970). In any case,
     due to data limitations, quarterly interpolations of annual income series,
     rather than quarterly measures of income, must be used in the estimation
     of inflation equations which employ quarterly inflation and money
     supply data.

11. J. Johnston, *Econometric Methods* (New York: McGraw-Hill Book Co.,
     1972).

12. P. Cagan, "The Monetary Dynamics of Hyperinflation," in Friedman, ed.,
     Studies in the Quantity Theory of Money (Chicago: University of Chicago
     Press, 1956), pp. 25-120.

13. Robert M. Solow, "Recent Controversies on the Theory of Inflation: An
     Eclectic View," in Stephen W. Rousseas, ed., *Proceedings of a Symposium
     on Inflation: Its Causes, Consequences and Control* (Wilton, Conn.: The
     Calven K. Kazanjian Economics Foundation Inc., 1969).

14. John Deaver, "The Chilean Inflation and the Demand for Money," David
     Meiselman, ed., *Varieties of Monetary Experience* (Chicago: University of
     Chicago Press, 1970).

15. Tobin, "Inflation and Employment," p. 9.

16. Christopher Sims, "Money, Income, and Causality," *American Economic
     Review,* September 1972.

17. Ibid., p. 543.

Chapter 4
The Testing of Latin American Structuralist and Monetarist Theories

1. Arnold Harberger, "The Dynamics of Inflation in Chile," in Carl Christ, ed., *Measurement in Economics: Studies in Mathematical Economics in Memory of Yehuda Grunfeld* (Stanford: Stanford University Press, 1963), pp. 219-250.
2. Dudley Seers, "A Theory of Inflation and Growth in Underdeveloped Economies based on the Experience of Latin America," *Oxford Economic Papers,* XIV, No. 2 (1962)
3. See Adolfo Diz, "Money and Prices in Argentina," in *Varieties of Monetary Experience,* David Meiselman, ed. (Chicago: University of Chicago Press, 1970), p. 112.
4. For the formulation of an Almon lag, see Shirley Almon, "The Distributed Lag Between Capital Appropriations and Expenditures," *Econometrica,* January 1965. A four-degree polynominal is estimated here.
5. Reichmann, in his unpublished Ph.D. dissertation, "Persistent Inflation and Macroeconomic Equilibrium — The Case of Chile: 1960-1969," (Harvard University, 1973), develops a model of inflation similar to that of Dutton, and which includes money supply as a function of past prices. He states: "With respect to lags we found in this quarterly model, that in general there is a tendency for fast adjustments: mean lags were 50 days for the rate of change of the money supply" (p. 5 of his summary).
6. Sims, "Money, Income, and Causality."
7. Carlos F. Diaz-Alejandro, *Essays on the Economic History of the Argentine Republic,* New Haven: Yale University Press, 1970.
8. For the method of computation and the resulting quarterly national income series for 1940-1958, see Harberger, "The Dynamics," pp. 249-250.
9. Diz, "Money and Prices in Argentina," in *Varieties of Monetary Experience,* David Meiselman, ed. (Chicago, University of Chicago Press, 1970), p. 128.
10. Direccion de Estadistica y Censos de la Republica de Chile (DEC): Serie de Investigaciones Muestrales, Muestra Nacional de Hogares, A 5. "Encuesta continua de mano de obra," November 1967-February 1968. pp. 20, 25.
11. This index and a discussion of its derivation are provided in the *Boletin Mensual,* No. 381, November 1959, pp. 755-758. Harberger's study employs the original CPI series for Santiago.

Selected Bibliography

Selected Bibliography

Books, Unpublished Theses, Pamphlets:

Alexander, Robert J. *Labor Relations in Argentina, Brazil, and Chile.* New York: McGraw-Hill Book Co., 1962.

_____. *Organized Labor in Latin America.* New York: The Free Press, 1965.

Baer, Werner and Kerstenetzky, Isaac, eds. *Inflation and Growth in Latin America.* Homewood, Ill.: Richard D. Irwin, 1964.

Bailey, Martin. *National Income and the Price Level.* New York: McGraw-Hill Book Co., 1962.

Corbo, Victor. *Inflation in Developing Countries.* Amsterdam: North-Holland, 1974.

Diaz-Alejandro, Carlos F. *Essays on the Economic History of the Argentine Republic.* New Haven: Yale University Press, 1970.

Edel, Matthew. *Food Supply and Inflation in Latin America.* New York: Praeger, 1969.

Fei, J. and Ranis, G. *Development of the Labor Surplus Economy.* Homewood, Ill.: Richard D. Irwin, 1964.

Ffrench-Davis, Ricardo. "Economic Policies and Stabilization Programs: Chile, 1952-1969." Unpublished Ph.D. dissertation, University of Chicago, 1971.

Garcia D'Acuncia, Eduardo. "Inflation in Chile: A Quantitative Analysis." Unpublished Ph.D. dissertation, Massachusetts Institute of Technology, 1964.

Garcia, Jorge and Freyhoffer, Hugo. *La Tasa Efectiva de la Inflacion en Chile entre 1961 y 1968.* Santiago, Chile: Universidad de Chile, Instituto de Economia y Planificacion, 1969.

Johnston, J. *Econometric Methods.* New York: McGraw-Hill Book Co., 1972.

Leijonhufvud, Axel. *On Keynesian Economics and the Economics of Keynes.* New York: Oxford University Press, 1968.

Little, Ian; Scitovsky, Tibor; and Scott, Maurice. *Industry and Trade in Some Developing Countries.* London: Oxford University Press, 1970.

Mamalakis, Markos and Reynolds, C. W. *Essays on the Chilean Economy.* Homewood, Ill.: Richard D. Irwin, 1965.

Maynard, Geoffrey. *Economic Development and the Price Level.* London: Macmillan, 1962.

Meiselman, David. ed. *Varieties of Monetary Experience.* Chicago: University of Chicago Press, 1970.

Pazos, Felipe. *Chronic Inflation in Latin America.* New York: Praeger, 1972.

Petras, James. *Politics and Social Forces in Chilean Development.* Berkeley and Los Angeles: University of California Press, 1969.

Phelps, Edmund S. *Inflation Policy and Unemployment Theory.* New York: W. W. Norton, 1972.

_____. et al. *Microeconomic Foundations of Employment and Inflation Theory.* New York: W. W. Norton, 1970.

Reichmann, Thomas. "Persistent Inflation and Macroeconomic Equilibrium – The Case of Chile: 1960-1969." Unpublished Ph.D. dissertation, Harvard University, 1973.

Schultz, Theodore. *Transforming Traditional Agriculture.* New Haven, Yale University Press, 1964.

Schultze, Charles. *Recent Inflation in the United States.* Study Paper No. 1 for the Joint Economic Committee of Congress, Washington, 1959.

Uri, Pierre with Kaldor, Nicholas; Ruggles, Richard; and Triffin, Robert. *A Monetary Policy for Latin America.* New York: Praeger, 1968.

Weintraub, Sidney. *A Theory of Monetary Policy under Wage Inflation.* St. Lucia, Australia: University of Queensland Press, 1974.

Articles

Andersen, Leonall and Carlson, Keith. "A Monetarist Model for Economic Stabilization." *Federal Reserve Bank of St. Louis Review* (April 1970).

Archibald, G. C. "The Structure of Excess Demand for Labor." In *Microeconomic Foundations of Employment and Inflation Theory,* pp. 212-223, edited by Edmund Phelps, et al. New York: W. W. Norton, 1970.

Baer, Werner. "The Inflation Controversy in Latin America: A Survey." *Latin American Research Review* II, No. 2 (Spring 1967).

Bailey, Martin. "The Creation of New Money in Chile, 1943-1956." Unpublisted manuscript.

Barro, Robert J. and Grossman, Herschel I., "A General Disequilibrium Model of Income and Employment," American Economic Review, V. 61 (March 1971) pp. 82-93.

Behrman, Jere. "The Determinants of the Annual Rates of Change of Sectoral Money Wages in a Developing Economy." *International Economic Review* (October 1971).

_____. "Short-Run Flexibility in a Developing Economy." *Journal of Political Economy* (1972) pp. 292-313.

_____. "Aggregative Market Responses in Developing Agriculture: The Postwar Chilean Experience." Chapter 2 in *Analysis of Development Problems: Studies of the Chilean Economy,* forthcoming.

_____ . "Cyclical Sectoral Capacity Utilization in a Developing Economy." Chapter 4 in *Analysis of Development Problems: Studies of the Chilean Economy,* forthcoming.

_____ . "Price Determination in an Inflationary Economy: The Dynamics of Chilean Inflation Revisited." Chapter 9 in *Analysis of Development Problems: Studies of the Chilean Economy,* forthcoming.

_____ . and Garcia, Jorge M. "A Study of Quarterly Nominal Wage Change Determinants in an Inflationary Developing Economy." Chapter 10 in *Analysis of Development Problems: Studies of the Chilean Economy,* forthcoming.

Cagan, P. "The Monetary Dynamics of Hyperinflation." *Studies in the Quantity Theory of Money,* pp. 25-120, edited by Friedman. Chicago: University of Chicago Press, 1956.

Campos, Roberto de Oliviera. "Two Views on Inflation in Latin America." *Latin American Issues,* pp. 69-73, edited by A. O. Hirschman, New York: Twentieth Century Fund, 1961.

_____ . "Monetarism and Structuralism in Latin America." *Leading Issues in Economic Development: Studies in International Poverty,* pp. 241-247, edited by G. M. Meier. New York: Oxford University Press, 1970.

Cauas, Jorge. "Stabilization Policy – The Chilean Case." *Journal of Political Economy* (July-August 1970).

Centro de Investigaciones Economicas, Universidad Catolica de Chile. "La Inflacion." *Cuadernos de Economia* (September 1970).

Cochrane, Susan H. "Structural Inflation and the Two-Gap Model of Economic Development." *Oxford Economic Papers* (November 1972).

Davis, Tom E. "Eight Decades of Inflation in Chile, 1879-1959: A Political Interpretation." *Journal of Political Economy* LXXI, No. 4 (August 1963).

Deaver, John. "The Chilean Inflation and the Demand for Money." In *Varieties of Monetary Experience,* edited by David Meiselman. Chicago: University of Chicago Press, 1970.

Diz Cesar, Adolfo. "Money and Prices in Argentina." *Varieties of Monetary Experience,* edited by David Meiselman. Chicago: University of Chicago Press, 1970.

Dutton, Dean S. "A Model of Self-Generating Inflation." *Journal of Money, Credit, and Banking* (May 1971).

Enthoven, Alain. "Monetary Disequilibria and the Dynamics of Inflation." *The Economic Journal* (June 1956) pp. 256-270.

Escobedo, Gilberto. "Formulating a Model of the Mexican Economy." *Federal Reserve Bank of St. Louis Review* (July 1973).

Fei, J. and Ranis, G. "A Theory of Economic Development." *American Economic Review* (September 1961).

Felix, David. "Monetarists, Structuralists and Import-Substituting Industrialization:

A Critical Appraisal." *Studies in Comparative International Development* I, No. 10 (1965).

——— . "Structural Imbalances, Social Conflict and Inflation." *Economic Development and Cultural Change* (January 1960).

——— . "An Alternative View of the Monetarist-Structuralist Controversy." *Latin American Issues,* edited by A. O. Hirschman. New York: Twentieth Century Fund, 1961.

Friedman, Benjamin, "Rational Expectations are Really Adaptive After All," unpublished discussion paper, Harvard University (February 1975).

Friedman, Milton. "The Role of Monetary Policy." *American Economic Review* (March 1968) pp. 1-17.

Gordon, Robert J., "Recent Developments in the Theory of Inflation and Unemployment," presented at the International Economics Association Conference on "Inflation Theory and Anti-Inflation Policy" Saltsjöbaden, Sweden (August 1975).

Grunwald, Joseph. "The 'Structuralist' School on Price Stability and Development: The Chilean Case," *Latin American Issues,* edited by A. O. Hirschman. New York: Twentieth Century Fund, 1961.

Harberger, Arnold. "The Dynamics of Inflation in Chile." *Measurement in Economics: Studies in Mathematical Economics in Memory of Yehuda Grunfeld,* pp. 219-250, edited by Carl Christ. Stanford: Stanford University Press, 1963.

——— . "El problema de la inflacion en American Latina." *CEMLA Boletin Mensual* XII, No. 6 (June 1966).

Harris, J. and Todaro, M. "Migration, Unemployment, and Development: A Two Sector Analysis." *American Economic Review* (March 1970).

Hirschman, A. O. "Inflation in Chile." *Journeys Toward Progress.* pp. 159-226. New York: The Twentieth Century Fund, 1963.

Koot, Ronald S. "A Test for Demand-Pull or Wage-Push Inflation: The Chilean Case." *Social and Economic Studies* XVII, No. 2 (June 1968).

——— . "Wage Changes, Unemployment, and Inflation in Chile." *Industrial and Labor Relations Review* (August 1969) pp. 568-575.

Kravis, Irving. "Trade as a Handmaiden of Growth: Similarities Between the 19th and 20th Centuries." University of Pennsylvania, Department of Economics Discussion Paper No. 105, 1968.

Lewis, W. A. "Economic Development with Unlimited Supplies of Labour." *The Manchester School* (May 1954).

Maynard, Geoffrey. "Inflation and Growth: Some Lessons to be Drawn from Latin American Experience." *Oxford Economic Papers* XIII, No. 2 (1961).

——— . "Inflation and Growth in Latin America." *Oxford Economic Papers* XV, No. 1 (1963).

_____ . and Rijckeghem, W. "Stabilization Policy in an Inflationary Economy – Argentina." *Development Policy: Theory and Practice*, pp. 207-238, edited by Papanek. Cambridge: Harvard University Press, 1968.

Mortensen, Dale. "A Theory of Wage and Employment Dynamics." *Microeconomic Foundations of Employment and Inflation Theory*, pp. 167-211, edited by Edmund Phelps, et al. New York: W. W. Norton, 1970.

Mueller, Marnie W. "Structural Inflation and the Mexican Experience." *Yale Economic Essays* E, No. 1 (Spring 1965).

Noyola, Juan. "El desarrollo economico y la inflacion en Mejico y otros paises latinoamericanos." *Investigacion Economica* 4 (1956).

Olivera, Julio H.G. "Aspectos Dinamicos de la Inflacion Estructural." *Desarrollo Economico*. Buenos Aires: October 1967.

_____ . "On Structural Inflation and Latin American 'Structuralism'." *Oxford Economic Papers* XVI, No. 3 (November 1964).

_____ . "On Passive Money." *Journal of Political Economy* (July-August 1970).

Phelps, Edmund. "Money Wage Dynamics and Labor Market Equilibrium." *Microeconomic Foundations of Employment and Inflation Theory*. New York: W. W. Norton, 1970.

Pinto, Anibal. "Raices Estructurales de la Inflacion en America Latina." *Trimestre Economico* XXXV, No. 1 (January 1968).

Prebisch, Raul. "Structural Vulnerability and Inflation." *Leading Issues in Economic Development: Studies in International Poverty*, pp. 238-241, edited by G. M. Meier. New York: Oxford University Press, 1970.

Ross, S.A. and Wachter, M. L. "The Pricing and Timing Decision of the Oligopoly Firm," *Quarterly Journal of Economics* (February 1975).

Seers, Dudley. "Normal Growth and Distortions: Some Techniques of Structural Analysis." *Oxford Economic Papers* XVI, No. 1 (1964).

_____ . "A Theory of Inflation and Growth in Underdeveloped Economies based on the Experience of Latin America." *Oxford Economic Papers* XIV, No. 2 (1962).

Sims, Christopher. "Money, Income, and Causality." *American Economic Review* (September 1972).

Solis, Leopoldo. "Mexican Economic Policy in the Post-War Period: The Views of Mexican Economists." *American Economic Review* (June 1971).

Solow, Robert M. "Recent Controversies in the Theory of Inflation: An Eclectic View." In *Proceedings of a Symposium on Inflation: Its Causes, Consequences and Control*, edited by Stephen Rousseas. Connecticut: Kazanjian Economics Foundation Inc., 1969.

Sunkel, Osvaldo, "Inflation in Chile: An Unorthodox Approach." *International Economic Papers* 10.

Thorp, Rosemary, "Inflation and Orthodox Economic Policy in Peru." *Bulletin of the Oxford University Institute of Economics and Statistics,* XXIX, No. 3 (August 1967).

Tobin, James, "Inflation and Unemployment." *American Economic Review* (March 1972) pp. 1-18.

Vogel, Robert, "The Dynamics of Inflation in Latin America, 1950-1969." *American Economic Review* (March 1974).

Wachter, Michael L., "Cyclical Variation in the Interindustry Wage Structure." *American Economic Review* V. 60 (March 1970) pp. 75-84.

_____ . "Wage Determination, Inflation, and the Industrial Structure." *American Economic Review* V. 63 (September 1973) pp. 675-692.

_____ and Susan Wachter, "Money Wage Inflation: The Endogeneity-Exogeneity Issue," in *Some Trends in Modern Economic Thought,* edited by Sidney Weintraub. Philadelphia: University of Pennsylvania Press, forthcoming.

Index

Index

Aggregate demand, 8, 12, 14, 15, 17, 20, 32-36, 43, 45, 63, 65, 70-71, 78, 80, 120, 121, 135-136, 137

Agricultural bottleneck hypothesis, xiii, 4-8, 10, 11, 42, 121, 135, 137

Almon lag, 91, 98, 103, 104, 149

Anti-inflation policies, xiii, 41, 121

Archibald, G. C., 65n, 144, 147

Argentina, 9, 12n, 13, 43, 51, 52, 53, 101-118 *passim,* 120-121, 137; data, 124; inflation equations, 103-115 *passim;* Sims test, 115-118 *passim*

Asamblea General Ordinaria de Accionistas (Mexico), 125

Autocorrelation, 87, 96, 99, 104

Banco Central de Chile, 121, 123

Banco Central de la Republica Argentina, 124

Banco Central do Brasil, 124-125

Banco de Mexico, 125

Barro, Robert J., 147

Behrman, Jere, 142

Blue-collar workers, 37

Boletin Estadistico (Argentina), 124

Boletin Mensual (Chile), 121, 123

Brazil, xiii, 42, 43, 101-118 *passim,* 120, 137; data, 124-125; inflation equations, 103-115 *passim;* Sims test, 115-118 *passim*

Buenos Aires, 124

Campos, Robert, xiii

Capital accumulation, 7, 8

Causality. *See* Sims test

Central banks, 35, 36n

Centro de Contas Nacionals (Brazil), 125

Chile, xiii, 2, 3, 4, 9, 13, 43, 45, 54, 55, 81-101, 104n, 114, 120, 137; data, 121-124, 149

Cochrane-Orcutt procedure, 87, 90, 91, 96, 97, 104, 108, 111, 115

Colombia, 43

Competitive/noncompetitive sectors, 16, 34, 37, 135

Conjuntura Economica (Brazil), 124, 125

Consumer price index (CPI), 45, 48, 82-83, 85, 98, 123

Corbo, Victorio, 13n, 104n

CORFO (Corporacion de Fomento de la Produccion, Chile), 122

Cost of holding money, 2, 3, 45, 47, 54, 62, 66, 84, 88n, 91, 95, 136

Cost of living, 10, 45, 46, 51, 124

Cost-push model, 10, 36-38, 46, 54, 56, 80

Costs: factor, 10; indirect, 16n; real, 74

Credit conditions, 35, 36n, 54

"Crowding-out," 61n

Cuentas Nacionales de Chile, 122

Data, 44; Argentina, Brazil, and Mexico, 101-118; Chile, 121-124

Deficit financing, 78

Demand-pull, 56, 85, 98, 99, 135, 136, 137; inflation, 59-80; measure of, 83-98; and quantity theory, 59-70; and reformulated structuralism, 70-75; variables, 82, 89, 97

Demand-shift inflation. *See* Schultze's model

Developed/developing economies, 17

Diaz-Alejandro, Carlos, 53-54, 55, 56, 101, 118, 143

161

About the Author

Susan M. Wachter is Assistant Professor of Finance at the Wharton School of the University of Pennsylvania. Formerly she taught at Bryn Mawr College. Dr. Wachter has published other works on the topic of inflation and is in the process of coediting a series of monographs dealing with current issues in economic policy.